WESTMINSTER BLUES

WESTMINSTER BLUES

Minor Chords by Julian Critchley

CARTOONS BY COLIN WHEELER

Elm Tree Books · London

312391

First published in Great Britain 1985
by Elm Tree Books/Hamish Hamilton Ltd
Garden House 57-59 Long Acre London WC2E 9JZ

British Library Cataloguing in Publication Data

Critchley, Julian
  Westminster blues.
  1. Great Britain — Politics and government
  — 1979-
  I. Title
  320'.092'4   JN237

  ISBN 0-241-11387-3

Typeset by Pioneer, East Sussex.
Printed in Great Britain by
Billing & Sons Ltd., Worcester.

To Humphrey and Angelica, without whose uncritical admiration and steadfast loyalty this book would never have been written

CONTENTS

Acknowledgements

Thanks to Tony Howard of the *Observer* and Russell Twisk of the *Listener* for permission to reprint articles of mine which originally appeared in those publications.

1 Shot in the Foot

In February 1980, I wrote an unsigned piece in the *Observer* attacking Mrs Thatcher and all her works. My confession of authorship, albeit a reluctant one, brought me instant fame, or notoriety, after fifteen years, on and off, on the Conservative back benches. The public row was short but intense with the right wing 'populars' in pursuit, and the 'fall-out', particularly among my local party supporters, was great. My *Observer* article was seen by the party loyalists as traitorous and deceitful; by the left as heroic and well-aimed; and by my friends as one of the better examples of how to shoot oneself in the foot. My error was not so much the views expressed in the piece, indeed they were widely shared even among Tories, but not to have signed the piece. As Hugh Stephenson wrote later in his book *Mrs Thatcher's First Year*, 'The impact of the article was somewhat reduced when Julian Critchley was forced to reveal that he was the author, for the substance of what he said was overtaken by the feeling that an anonymous article was an underhand art form. There was no doubt, however, that he was expressing the views of a substantial part of the Tory Party in Parliament.'

Why then did I write it? And, having decided to put pen to paper, why did I not sign it?

Six months previously I had gone to my cousin's house in Nether Stowey in Somerset to spend the month of August. I had been re-elected as Conservative MP for Aldershot in the June '79 election but had received no invitation to join the Government. I was forty-eight, had served in four Parliaments (for Rochester and Chatham as well as Aldershot) and whereas not 'on' the front bench in opposition, I had spoken from it on broadcasting and media matters, deputising, more often than not, for the absent Willie Whitelaw. I was

Chairman of the party's Media Committee, and a Vice-Chairman of the Defence Committee, posts from which Ministers are traditionally recruited. I had doubts about Margaret but they had not been made public.

I tramped the Quantock Hills pondering my future. I had clearly come to a turning point. I had not gone into politics as an extension of my sense of social obligation as did many of the more traditional members of our party; I was, and always had been, a careerist, in that I would have welcomed office, particularly in the defence field, and had not totally acquiesced in the promotion of my juniors. Had Ted Heath won in '74, it might have been different, but that was old hat. I thought that the care I had taken during the seventies had overlain the reputation I had won for myself in the early sixties as a rebel. But I had received no telephone call from Downing Street in the aftermath of our triumph in June and it seemed highly unlikely that any future invitation would be forthcoming. I was, indeed, too long in the tooth to be made a Parliamentary Secretary and an appointment to Minister of State level would have been even less likely. The door had finally closed.

I had a choice. I could soldier on giving loyal and largely silent support to a Government the radical fervour of which I would increasingly come to dislike, in the hope of a knighthood as a consolation prize; or I could play the part of a *franc-tireur*, a free spirit ranging the back benches, using my voice and my pen to strike an individual note. The role might be fun but it certainly would be hazardous, for there would always be the danger of defenestration or the abandonment of the Member by the Aldershot party activists who, if forced to place a premium upon party loyalty, would be more generous than me. I would be breaking to the left in Conservative Party terms, something which is always harder to do than from the right. Party activists tend to be more sympathetic to more robust attitudes, such as capital punishment for Blacks. Sitting on some rock overlooking the Bristol Channel, in a mood of gloomy resolution, I concluded that whereas I was a major minor figure in our party, I would set out to become a minor major figure within it. As an ambition, it was modest enough; I walked back to the car and drove back to the village determined to flex my muscles.

In the autumn of 1979 I put myself at the head of those Tory backbenchers who took strong objection to the proposed cuts in the External Services of the BBC which are funded by a grant in aid through the Foreign and Commonwealth Office's vote. My campaign was conducted in a way which offended the Whips' Office and the Chief Whip, Michael Jopling, in particular. Dissident backbenchers are supposed to take the Whips into their confidence and to keep them informed as to intention: a curious arrangement, to which I was not a party, which gave to the Government a sizeable advantage. Instead, I announced my intention of fighting the proposed cuts on *The World This Weekend* to which the unhappy Jopling was listening while sipping sherry before lunch at his mother-in-law's house. I am afraid my declaration of war came between him and the roast beef of Old England.

During the week that followed we arranged to meet and, when we did so, passed a *mauvais quart d'heure:* I told him I thought the cuts were parsimonious and that I would contest them with all the weapons at my disposal. 'What are they?' he asked.'The media,' I replied. It was the first time I had ever spoken to Michael Jopling, who had been a surprise choice as Government Chief Whip. In Ted Heath's Government he had been a junior Minister of Agriculture. He is a large, good-natured man, a friend of William Whitelaw's, and a 'traditional Tory'. He drives motorbikes with his very pretty wife perched on the pillion.

I had thought that I had at least imposed my personality upon the great man but I was soon to be disappointed. It so happened that Michael Jopling went up to Peter Tapsell in the Aye Lobby the same evening, and, placing his hand upon his shoulder, said, 'Julian, you and I must continue our conversation.' Tapsell was very angry indeed, and upbraided the unhappy Jopling, but I was hugely entertained. Tapsell and I have been receiving each other's letters and messages for years, for there is a physical resemblance, but so hilarious a misunderstanding soon became common knowledge. Jopling and I did not 'continue our conversation', and we did not meet until I had acknowledged the authorship of my anonymous article, an occasion when he believed himself to have regained the advantage.

3

My successful campaign against the cuts in the External Services whetted my appetite: more than one hundred Tory backbenchers had signed my Early Day Motion which I had placed upon the Order Paper, and a Friday afternoon adjournment debate in which three of us had taken five minutes each to demolish the arguments deployed by Peter Blaker, who was plainly unhappy in his role as defender of the indefensible, had caused a stir. The media relished the first 'Tory revolt' of the new Parliament and, at the end of the day, we won on points, as the threatened cuts were themselves reduced. It was a minor but not insignificant success at a time when Mrs Thatcher's Government was riding high. I re-loaded my gun and waited for a target to present itself.

I had not long to wait. The early months of Mrs Thatcher's first Government were set to martial music: brass, over which her shrill contralto could be heard urging friend and foe to go over the top. There is a quality to that gritty voice which, when combined with a fierce and unrelenting glare, and the repetition of the obvious, amounts to the infliction of pain. Her supporters seemed to relish her exhortations: those of us who had doubts cringed as she continued remorselessly to trample upon our susceptibilities. The genie had escaped the bottle and swallowed the cork.

Her behaviour at the Dublin Summit in January 1980 when she publicly scolded Giscard and Schmidt and demanded the return of 'our money', shocked the pro-Europeans in the Tory party and cheered the 'antis'. Whatever the merits of the demand for a reduced subscription to a club which we had joined late in the day and after three sets of negotiations culminating in a successful referendum campaign, the effect of her scolding upon those whom she was obliged to persuade, as well as upon the spectators, seemed as futile as it was unpleasing. There was a great row which took place largely behind the scenes in which Establishment figures threw up their hands, although a Foreign and Commonwealth Office spokesman was obliged to comment that it was not the function of British diplomacy simply to be polite to foreigners. As time went on the Foreign Office became the target for much of the Prime Minister's public and private disapproval, staffed as it appeared to her

4

to be, by the *déracinés* who did not share her more robust view of British interests. In truth, she was confronted by subtle men and women, used to expressing dissent in graduated terms, and for whom the truth was necessarily many-sided. It was not to be long before our diplomats became the last persecuted minority in Britain.

I was angry and determined to write an article which would express the anxieties of many of my friends. I was tempted to emulate the series of pieces which appeared in *The Times* in the mid sixties under the signature of 'A Conservative'. These 'turnovers', appearing on consecutive days, were an attack upon the Conservative Party policies of the fifties and sixties, and, in particular, upon the policies of Harold Macmillan. Their appearance caused a stir, and some innocent fun, as the newspapers and others speculated as to the identity of the author. The pieces were a brilliantly argued demolition of the basis of post-war Conservatism, 'the politics of consensus', and in the search for a name to put to them, most people did not look beyond that of Enoch Powell. But Mr Powell denied authorship, and the fuss died down. The articles were the first shot in a barrage of dissent which, ten years later, Sir Keith Joseph in particular articulated without disguise. And Mrs Thatcher was, of course, Sir Keith's candidate to challenge Edward Heath.

I suggested the idea to John Cole, who was then the *Observer's* political correspondent. He told me the paper would take one piece, unsigned, if that was what I wished. Unwisely, I did not take the advice of my friends. I did ask Sir Nigel Fisher, who was sympathetic to my point of view, and his advice was to publish anonymously least I offend my constituency party. Sadly, David Walder, who had been my closest friend in the House, had died suddenly two years before: his opinion would most certainly have been sought. As secrecy was of the essence I was reluctant to canvass further views. I wrote the piece and sent it to the *Observer* and it appeared on Sunday 16 February 1980.

Why Tories must halt the charge of Margaret's Light Brigade

LORD CHALFONT recounted last week the view of a Tory MP who had compared the progress of the Government with that of the Crimean War —' but with this difference: Florence Nightingale is leading the Charge of the Light Brigade and Lord Cardigan is tending the s i c k and wounded.'

As a judgment it is unkind, disloyal, pertinent and funny. It is also indicative of the growing disquiet, felt both in the Cabinet and on the back benches, with the pace and direction of Mrs Thatcher's Light Brigade.

It is a matter both of policy a n d personality. Mrs Thatcher is didactic, tart and obstinate. Her economic policies are 'Thatcherite' rather than Conservative, for her Treasury team have placed the Public Sector Borrowing Requirement upon a pedestal, despite there being no evident causal relationship over the past decade between the growth of the PSBR and the growth of the money supply (M3).

We are suffering from ' A '

A Conservative MP warns his Leader that A-level economics will lead their party to disaster.

level economics. In consequence of this new ideology, economics have been elevated above politics in an almost Marxist fashion, and it cannot be long before the Conservative Party will be obliged to pay the price. As the cannonade increases, so must the casualties.

It is not enough for Sir Keith Joseph to seek martyrdom in the valleys of South Wales. What is wanted is a relaxation of the Government's cash limits. The steel strike should never have been allowed to take place. Following the miners' settlement of 22 per cent, it was utterly unrealistic to suppose that Bill Sirs—a moderate leader of a union which has not struck for 50 years—could ever have sold to his members a package that contained an initial 2 per cent increase, factory closures and redundancies on a large scale.

The failings of the steel industry are common knowledge, but it is not enough to rehearse them; disapproval gets nobody back to work. Whatever the economic price to be paid—and as stocks run down, the effect of the strike will become more severe—the political cost to the Government is too high. Labour relations have become inflamed, as they were bound to do.

The Cabinet has been divided over the best way to strengthen the Employment Bill in response to public pressure, and Mr Prior, who leads the forces of light, has been hard put to hold the line. The final irony is that a Government which is prone to charge in all directions at once has come under fire from its noisiest supporters for lack of moral fibre.

We have been no more successful abroad. We were defeated at the Battle of Dublin where, without adequate preparation, and with the wrong tone of voice, the Prime Minister took on her allies and lost. Perhaps she should have behaved a little more like Helen of Troy and less like Hector. It is certainly true that our subscription to a club which we took 15 years to join is now uncomfortably high, but that is not the fault of our fellow-members.

Recession in Europe has kept the farmers on the land, while at home trade union barricades and managerial inefficiencies have combined to depress our industrial performance. But the one thousand million pounds was never 'our' money: it belonged to the Community of which we are a member, and Mrs Thatcher will now do well to settle for half that amount. The Government should never have cast the Community as the scapegoat for our economic ills.

The trouble is that the monetarists have been put in charge. They man the Treasury, from whose rococo towers they call for yet more cuts across the board, a particularly foolish form of economy in which good causes suffer more than bad, and the political consequences of which are tiresome and unnecessary. The country sees a need for a reduction of government spending, as does the Conservative Party, but not all the 'victims' are equally deserving : waste and extravagance are legitimate targets ; but the British Council, the external services of the BBC, the arts, rural school bus fares and the sick and mentally-handicapped, are not.

There is anxiety within the Cabinet at the Prime Minister's taste for charging uphill (as one Cabinet Minister put it : ' The Prime Minister flies by the seat of her pants '), but the moderates stand at the periphery, engaged upon their separate tasks, unable so far to combine effectively to bring about a change in economic policy. Sir Ian Gilmour's recent speech may mark the first swallow of the summer.

The moderates on the back benches, who probably constitute the majority, have kept an embarrassed silence, torn between loyalty and irritation. We sorely miss Reggie Maudling, who maintained an intelligent critique of monetarist fads and fashions which our masters pass off as Conservatism. Maudling was never one to believe in the sacred flame, and there are many of us left who have no wish to be consumed by it.

At first there was no apparent reaction. The article was not mentioned in Monday's newspapers, and although one or two people asked if I was responsible for it, little or nothing else was said.

On the following Saturday I returned from a Conservative Group for Europe conference at Brandon Hall in Warwickshire having made one of my better speeches. All was still until the mid-afternoon of Sunday when I was rung by the diary of the *Daily Mail*. He wanted to know whether I was the 'Julian' whom Sir John Junor, the editor of the *Sunday Express* (and knighted in January 1980 by Margaret Thatcher) had referred to as the author of the anonymous attack upon the Prime Minister in last Sunday's *Observer*. I said I was not. No doubt the *Mail* had already spoken to the other two Julians: Mr Julian Amery, the Brighton Imperialist; and Sir Julian Ridsdale, the Member for Harwich.

I had scarcely recovered from that bombshell when the telephone rang again. This time it was Commander Mike Chappell, a constituent who lived in Darby Green, and who was, together with his wife, Esther, a personal friend as well as a keen supporter of the party. He demanded to know whether I was the 'guilty party' of John Junor's column. I admitted to being so. Whereas I could bring myself to lie to the newspapers, I was not prepared to do so when challenged by friends. Mike, not unreasonably perhaps, gave me a dose of the rough edge of his tongue.

I was in a very tight spot. I rang Anthony Buck, a friend in the House whom I would have done better to consult before putting pen to paper. He is a Queen's Counsel. He advised me to come clean: to ring back the *Mail's* diary and admit to my authorship. This I did. I also telephoned the President of the local Tories, General Tom Foulkes, and the chairman, Jack Bedser, and gave them what must have been unwelcome news. I was then in the unenviable position of having to wait for the storm to burst, a sense of evil anticipation which was not helped by the knowledge that I had foolishly made a difficult situation far worse.

The explosion, when it came, reverberated around my head. It is impossible to calculate accurately the extent of the response of the press; an outrageous word or deed can pass almost without comment, depending to some extent upon the pressures of events upon available space; in my case the papers seemed empty of more significant news. The *Mail* was scathing in its diary report, and my telephone started to ring. I hurried to London to defend myself on ITN's midday news. My only course was to stick to my guns, but to admit that it would have been wiser to have signed. My description of Mrs Thatcher as 'didactic, tart and obstinate' seemed to have shocked hardened commentators of the political scene, although I see no reason five years later to revise my opinion. Perhaps it was simply that I was the first to say what many were beginning to think? She is still, I am sorry to say, tart, obstinate and didactic.

The story continued into the Tuesday with the rest of the press joining in. The most abusive volley came later, predictably enough from the *Sunday Express*. John Junor, that unamiable old Scot, beat me about my head with his claymore, calling upon my constituency party to disown me, and describing me as fit only to be 'the second pianist in a whorehouse'. I considered using that as a title for this book. It was not the first time, or the last, that the *Sunday Express*, usually in its 'Crossbencher' column, which was once required reading, has tried to come between me and my supporters. It has yet to succeed.

My reception in the House ranged from the mutely hostile to the hilarious as ancient enemies warmed their hands at the fires of my discomfiture while my friends, regretting perhaps that I had made an ass of myself, stood me drinks. It was not long before I was once again summoned to attend upon a more confident Michael Jopling. This time he knew who I was. 'It's very off-side,' he kept on saying. He said he had known who had written it by the end of the week. He would not say how. 'We have our methods of finding out.' He went on to say that it would be a long time, if at all, before the party would forgive me. In effect, he rang down the curtain.

I learnt later that the Whips' Office, at Downing Street's prompting, had set out to discover who the offender might be. They drew up a short list on which my name appeared together with those of Peter Tapsell, John Watson and John Selwyn Gummer. It would not have been too difficult to draw up such a list. The author was likely to be a dissident backbencher with no love for the Government's economic policy, and a writer with a turn of phrase, e.g. 'we are suffering from "A" level economics.' I was told much later by Morrison Halcrow, who was then, and still is, the *Daily Telegraph's* deputy editor, that it was the view of Jock Bruce Gardyne, at that time a loyalist backbencher, that it could only be Critchley, 'as it was so well written', a view expressed at a *Telegraph* editorial meeting.

I was, of course, quite unconscious of these acts of detection. Michael Jopling's source could well have been Lord Barnetson, who was at the time the Chairman of the *Observer* and an admirer of Mrs Thatcher. I did receive a letter signed 'Tory Minister', written upon blue House of Commons writing paper, which claimed that I had been 'shopped' by Adam Raphael, who was an *Observer* lobby correspondent, but I doubt if that were the case. Barnetson is likely, but it is more probable that the whips arrived at their conclusion by process of elimination. I was not challenged as to authorship: they might well have done so in the case of the other names appearing on their short list.

For a fortnight I was snowed under with letters. One third were literate and favourable, most of the rest abusive or illiterate. But there were some disturbing ones from the more educated end of the constituency. My officers publicly defended my right to criticise adversely Government policy while deploring my anonymity, a device which enabled them to hold the line against those who would have tried to censure me. The most hostile branch was Crondall, the smartest village in East Hampshire, where I was told I would not be welcome. The Chairman sent a letter of support to the Prime Minister; his Vice-Chairman immediately sent another in which he came to my support. Both letters were made public in the village. At the end of a hectic fortnight the editor of the *Aldershot News* wrote a leader column in which he wondered what on earth all the fuss was about. I was grateful to him.

At the end of February, the Opposition called a Censure Debate on the Government's economic policies and I was called. I made what I think was a good speech, and the

CRONDALL

House filled as I spoke. I repeated much of what I had written in the *Observer*. Roy Hattersley sent me a note saying it was 'brave and elegant', and so did Robert Atkins from our side. It was reported in every paper with the *Financial Times* being especially complimentary: 'The most articulate of the Tory "wets". ' I had felt pretty sick with apprehension all day and as soon as my ordeal was over I left the chamber for a drink and a sandwich. I ran straight into Mrs Thatcher who grasped me by the wrist and said how sorry she was to have missed my speech and that 'everything would be all right'. Did she mean my umbraged constituents or her economic policies? It was a kind gesture in the circumstances.

This was not the end of the affair. Unfortunately for me the timing of my escapade could not have been more unfortunate, for the first Wednesday in March is traditionally the date for the Aldershot Conservatives' largest private meeting, the Annual Women's Conference, held over lunchtime on the well-sprung floor of the Aldershot Officers

Club where Joan Hunter Dunn had danced the night away. It was an occasion when we were visited briefly by a Cabinet Minister. This year I had persuaded Angus Maude, a devoted Thatcherite, who had been rescued by her from a long life spent upon the back benches, and whose task in her Cabinet was to worry about the presentation of Government policy. He told the press that he would not be coming after all.

I had also invited Sir Paul Bryan, a senior backbencher and a director of Granada Television, to speak after lunch on the problems of the media. (I was at the time the Chairman of the Tory Party's Media Committee.) He said he would turn up, not wishing to embarrass the local party. But he made it a condition that I should not sit on the platform beside him. I had little choice but to accept his condition. In Maude's stead I managed to persuade Stephen Murray of the IBA to come and speak in the morning.

Maude's snub rekindled the interest of the press, who turned up to what is usually a private and often pedestrian meeting in large numbers. They must have been pretty bored but at the end of the afternoon their patience was rewarded. I was obliged to read out a statement apologising for my original article and for not signing it, and re-affirming my support for the Government. I managed also to include a paragraph stressing my right to speak out against policies of which I disapproved. The next morning's *Times* spoke of errant Member eating humble pie. It was for me the worst part of the whole affair.

There was a silver lining. John Biffen, learning of my plight upon Maude's withdrawal, published a statement in which he said he would be happy to speak for me 'anywhere, anytime'. It was a magnificent gesture of friendship from a Cabinet Minister who had long admired the Prime Minister and was no 'wet'. It was typical of him. As for Angus Maude, all I could do was remind him gently in the Smoking Room of the occasion in the sixties when he had been sacked from the Shadow Cabinet by Ted Heath for writing an attack upon party policy in the pages of the *Spectator*. *Autres temps*...

To sum up, the whole exercise was a foolish mistake. I would have done better to moderate my criticism of Mrs Thatcher and sign the piece. But Norman Lamont, a junior Minister, said that the whole affair 'had been the making of me'. Apparently, I had moved from relative obscurity to relative fame. It put an end to any hopes I might still have secretly entertained of getting office, at least under a Thatcher regime. It had damaged my standing among the stauncher Tories in Aldershot, although making me something of a hero to the left wing. A strange girl stopped me in New Palace Yard and said how much she admired my courage. But I had not really been brave at all, for my generalship owed more to Nivelle than to Foch.

There is a Spanish proverb which says 'the blow that does not break you, makes you'. I took care to mend my fences locally and my re-adoption as candidate took place without a hitch three years later. But I also felt freer than ever before to speak out against both the style and substance of many of Mrs Thatcher's policies. I was my own man.

2   'Such Nice Girls . . .'

The road that eventually led me to Westminster, to the Palace of Varieties, passed through Hampstead, Paris and Oxford before I managed in 1957 to be adopted as Tory candidate for the marginal seat of Rochester and Chatham.

At the age of 18 I had joined the Hampstead Young Conservatives. I had nothing better to do. In the forties the YCs were 'the largest political youth movement in the world', and I was persuaded to march with them through the streets of Hammersmith — Churchill took the salute, perched precariously on the narrow balcony of the local Conservative club — chanting the by-election slogan 'Get Fell in'. In the event he did not. Mr Attlee had little to fear from the YCs *en marche;* despite cries of 'fascists' from onlookers, we strolled cheerfully enough through the streets of Hammersmith, raising a cheer as we passed the palais de danse, the well-washed, short-back-and-sides, tweed-jacketed sons of the middle-middle class and jolly tennis club girls.

I was waiting to be called up for my National Service and living at home in my parents' house at Swiss Cottage. I spent my time in the pictures, seated guiltily in the palatial gloom of the Odeon, Swiss Cottage watching Alan Ladd and William Bendix, and lusting with a fierce, virginal passion after Gloria Grahame. It was 1949, a shabby year of peeling paint work, weed-filled bomb sites, food rationing, a dull continuation of war-time austerity and Government exhortation. It was a dull, unconfident morning.

I became a Tory not from conviction but from pleasure. There were, as my mother put it, 'so many nice girls', Pams, Susans and Marions, hairdressers and shop assistants, trim but respectable. It was true that we were often harangued by Geoffrey Finsberg, at the time Hampstead's rising hope, but it was a price we were pleased to pay. We spent Saturday afternoons playing tennis on municipal courts, the evenings dancing decorously in the leafy pavilions of Haverstock Hill, eating cold pork pie, pickles and potato salad. Then the long walk home across a silent Hampstead to NW6 and fumbling and unsatisfactory good-nights. The girls were sweet, but stern and unbending.

We did our bit politically. We conspired successfully to replace Charles Challen by Henry Brooke as MP for the borough of Hampstead. I attended a noisy meeting at the

Embassy Theatre and cast my vote, as instructed, against Challen. On Tuesday evenings we sat in a dingy room at College Crescent decorated with posters of Walter Eliot and 'Captain' Macmillan (part of a series entitled 'The Tory Team'), listening politely to a speaker. It was a pretty painless

indoctrination. We were not encouraged to think, still less to write. It was not our pens that were wanted, but our feet. At elections we went canvassing, climbing the front steps of tall, grubbily stuccoed houses in Belsize Park, pressing the battery of bells, marking up the doubtfuls by the light of the street lamps. Sometimes expeditions were mounted into enemy territory, such as Kilburn or Kentish Town. In the 1950 general election we were continuously engaged, the foot-soldiers of the counter-revolution, canvassing with the girl of the moment, deployed around the marginal seats of London, ready to do or die. We had the time of our lives.

In November 1950 I fell sick with polio. Only a fortnight before, I had attended my medical and had been passed fit for National Service. The examination was held in some vast Victorian barracks in Acton. I stood naked in a long line down which marched an officer and the doctor. The officer stopped when he reached me and said, 'I can see you are a public school boy. What regiment are ye joinin'?' I said I did not know. I was told to follow him into an office, where I agreed to put my name down for the Greenjackets. I now know what it is that the 'Black Mafia' must have in common.

When I recovered I took my limp to Paris, the Greenjackets having been sent to the war in Korea. Susan, Marion and Pam saw me off from Victoria. I was to attend the Sorbonne. I had a return second class ticket, an allowance of £30 a month, a duffle-coat, a credit in school certificate French and was still a virgin. Philip Larkin is not the first of the 'fouled up generation'.

Paris in 1950 was still the city of Marcel Carné. The cafés were all zinc tops and brown paint, the buses had open platforms at the back, and the taxis were snub-nosed Renaults. The city danced to the sound of klaxons. Juliette Greco was singing in the Rue des Saints Pères, Pierre Mendès-France was encouraging his compatriots to drink milk, and Eisenhower was exhorted 'to go home'. It was a moveable feast but I did at least go one better than Hemingway. I set up a branch of the Paris Young Conservatives. So severe a challenge to the institutions of the Fourth Republic passed unnoticed in France but a report in the *Continental Daily Mail* of the inaugural meeting was picked up by the British press. Lord Woolton sent us a message of support. Under French law we were obliged to register as a political organisation, an act of a day which was met by bureaucratic incredulity. We were clearly mad.

We held our meetings in the drawing room flat owned by an émigré White Russian banker whose naturalised son was a YC. We opened the proceedings by planning to go dancing at Mimi Pinson, and to spend Saturday afternoon playing tennis at Roland Garros: we ended by necking. We addressed no envelopes, invited no speakers and knocked on no doors. It would not have met with Geoffrey Finsberg's approval.

I said earlier that I had become a Conservative for pleasure and not by conviction. My parents were strong Conservatives although they took no part in politics. My father is a neurologist, the son of a clerk in the Bristol Gas Works, the scholarship son of respectable lower-middle class parents whose robust Conservatism was entirely predictable: my mother was the fifth child of a Shropshire railway worker killed in an accident on the line in 1902. The Morris's were English in a border county where the Welsh were Liberal, and my mother's family had touched their caps to, and voted for, generations of Mores who had represented South Shropshire in the Tory interest. In the late seventies, my wife and I went to stay with Jasper More at Linley, the first of the 'Morris's' to do so. I was thus a child of the professional middle class, sent first to a prep school and later to Shrewsbury; first generation public school, very conventional in outlook, a Tory, or something like it, on both sides. I would not have been encouraged to join the Young Socialists, or even the Young Liberals. I was quite simply, a Conservative conscript.

But I became interested in politics; something from all those talks, delivered by visiting speakers from Central Office at College Crescent, and the twice-yearly pep talks delivered by Henry Brooke (a very dull speaker, indeed) fired my enthusiasm, and elections, and even electioneering, became a passion. When I went up to Pembroke College, Oxford in October 1951, I wanted to become a journalist and a politician.

I drove up to Oxford on my Vespa scooter. The university

authorities insisted that it carry a small green lamp. This aid to identification, which had been enshrined in a clause in some 1920s Traffic Act, was a matter of concern to police forces beyond Oxford, and I was frequently stopped and reprimanded. In Oxford, the garages had long conspired to thwart the proctors. When I bought my first car, a 1937 Model Y Ford, from a Hertfordshire chicken farmer, the lamp was fixed in such a way that it did not shine when one drove with dipped headlights. I was made welcome at Pembroke and given a large room on the first floor, facing Tom Tower. I bought a bottle of sherry, a Renoir reproduction, and placed an order for *France-Soir* to be delivered daily. It was Paris that had made me insufferable.

I had an income from my father, through deed of covenant, of £8 a week, which kept me comfortably in a state of disguised unemployment. In Christ Church my income would have gone unremarked; in Pembroke I was rich. As I wanted to go into politics I had chosen to read PPE. I would have done better to read history, which has since become a passion.

I wore a selection of my father's suits, which were expensively tailored and magisterial in style. I sported bow ties, and, in the privacy of my room, an old silk dressing-gown of my father's. I was intolerable and it was not long before I made friends with Michael Heseltine. I remembered him from Shrewsbury. At Pembroke he was cropped and provincial-looking but he was quick to acquire that patina which the nation has come to know and love. He, too, was in search of fame, and we joined forces.

He was a good ally. I had never met anyone quite as ambitious. From the start we sat in our rooms before the fire, over which were displayed our invitations, sipping sweet sherry, and, safe from the autumnal winds, we charted our course. We would share out the offices of the University Conservative Association between us and then take the Union by storm. The college seemed small beer; the university was to be our stage.

We promptly attended all the meetings of OUCA and drew attention to ourselves by question and comment. This, we believed, would quickly lead to our election to the committee. We would then be able to rely upon the

Conservative vote in Union elections; for the Presidency was the object of the exercise. But we had forgotten 'the House'. The Oxford Tories consisted in the main of men from Magdalen and Christ Church whose fair hair flopped over their foreheads and who talked of horses. They were the gents and we were the players. Pembroke was, after all, a dim sort of place — a 'place where they all wear college blazers and ties', and Michael's dialectic and my father's suits did not disguise the fact that we were bounders. We stood for election at the end of our first term but 'the House', the members of which have been described somewhere as spending their days 'either buggering, beagling or falling off their seats', organised against us, and scores of unknown young men in brown trousers came out to cast their votes. Old England had been mobilised against the New

The gents were decent but not very bright. Lloyd George was not far out when he described the Tories as 'the stupid party'. We just went one better and announced the formation of a rival Conservative Association to be called 'The Blue Ribbon Club'. The inaugural meeting drew a large audience, in the main from the humbler colleges, and Michael was elected President and I was elected Secretary, a relationship which has been sustained ever since. But we were on our way.

I soon stumbled. I invited Henry Brooke, the only prominent Tory whom I knew, up to speak, but it was reported to me the evening before he was due that the Minister had been spotted in the Randolph gloomily picking at a chop. He had come only to find an empty hall and had left by the last train.

Pembroke was in those days a bit dim, but very pretty. Homes Dudden was the Master, but he was in his nineties and bedridden. His functions were carried out by the Senior Tutor, R. B. McCallum, a delightful lowland Scot, who taught politics. He had been the author of a book on the 1945 election, an act of scholarship which has spawned any number of imitations. I once asked him his opinion of Richard Crossman, who, in a velvet dinner jacket and black suede shoes, was a frequent and brilliant speaker at the Union. 'A dreadful man' was his reply. 'He has debauched his undergraduates.' A Liberal of the Asquith school, he once told us why he never joined the Labour Party. 'The Labour Party is not a party, it is a movement. I could never join a movement.' I was taught economics by Neville Ward Perkins, who introduced me to Samuelson, Kaldor and Keynes. Sad to say, he was still young when he died in the fifties. A Mr McNab did his best to teach me moral philosophy.

In the early fifties Oxford was still reeling from the effect of a glittering generation of undergraduates who had come up at the end of the war. Battle-scarred captains had made way for National Service second lieutenants and boys straight from school. The talk at the bar of the Union was of the great men who had just gone down. Robin Day and Jeremy Thorpe, Peter Kirk and Ken Tynan: they had burnt so brightly we felt we could not compete. Shirley Catlin was spoken of as the first woman Prime Minister but Margaret Roberts was never mentioned.

The Oxford Union was to be the proving ground on which our ambition would be tested to destruction. Its reputation as a Temple to Precocity was worldwide, its membership large and the subscription low. In consequence, it was always in debt. Canvassing for election was forbidden but nothing could prevent the competing peacocks from displaying their plumage.

To succeed in politics it is important to speak well and Michael Heseltine and I enrolled in the speaker's classes which were held weekly in the offices of the Oxford City Tories. We were taught by a Mrs Stella Gatehouse, the wife of a Banbury parson who gave us a theme such as 'set the people free', culled from Conservative Central Office, which we would then expound to a captive audience of the ambitious. After a week or two, we were allowed out; free to drive into the country in order to address a women's afternoon meeting of village Tories. Two-up on a Vespa scooter, we drove the dusty lanes of Oxfordshire and Berks in search of dingy halls: on arrival we would rehearse the speech scheduled to be delivered at the Union that Thursday evening, treating an undemanding audience of retired gentlefolk and farm labourers' wives to ten minutes of ancient argument and even older jokes. They never seemed to mind. After twenty-five minutes or so, there would be a rattle of tea cups at the sound of which we had been trained by Stella

Gatehouse to sit down — a habit which I have yet to break.

At the Union I was elected top of the Library Committee, the first step on the ladder, but although I was runner-up, I never made the Standing Committee, which was necessary to stand for office. I never overcame my nerves. Michael had no such problems, and, climbing the ladder, was elected to the Presidency at the end of the summer term of his third year. He was then a curiously wooden speaker with little of the flair he has shown since, particularly at the Party Conference. He was picked less for his wit than for his nous, for as Treasurer he had saved the Union by turning its cellars into a nightclub. Always the manager, Michael was given a doctor's mandate to turn profit into loss, and for a time he did, with the generous help of Lady Docker.

Whom else do I remember? Gerald Kaufman, who told me that, despite his vast literary output, Churchill was no intellectual. He was clever and acid-tongued, believing then, as now, that Michael Heseltine was too good to be true. David Hughes, who married Mai Zetterling and wrote novels; Anthony Thwaite, who edited *Isis* and who published a short story of mine. Jeremy Isaacs, Scots and saturnine; Paddy Mayhew, patrician and quick-witted; Tyrrell Burgess, who rose to the top of the Union more swiftly than anyone else; and Anthony Howard, who could speak as well as he could write. I cannot recall meeting either Rupert Murdoch or Malcolm Fraser.

Then there was Peter Tapsell, who was a prominent member of the Labour Club, while Bryan Magee, a gifted intellectual, was a successful President of the Union. Maggie Smith performed at the New Theatre, Patrick Dromgoole produced for OUDS, and *The Mousetrap* began its out of London run. Nemone Lethbridge started a magazine called *Couth.*

In a search for fame, we neglected our college and our books. But not our pleasure. Michael and I would dine most evenings at 'Long John's', a restaurant owned by a Mr Silver, who had served in the army during the war with Michael's father. In return for our patronage, we were permitted to eat at half price, in the hope that other undergraduates would abandon dinner in hall. Michael would take from his pocket an envelope and draw upon it a chart of his progress within and beyond Oxford.'Downing Street' was the goal towards which he strove; the date, the 1990s.

In 1953 the Festival Ballet came to the New Theatre with a performance of *Scheherazade*. We spotted in the Oxford *Mail* an advertisement for extras, for 'guardsmen' to perform on stage for four nights at ten bob a night. We turned up and were kitted out in Wellingtons, turbans and wooden swords, our task to wait — in the company of half a dozen others who seemed to be South African rugger players and drunk — in the wings during the final act, until, at the bidding of an old queen who dropped his handkerchief as a signal, we would charge on stage and massacre the ballet girls (and boys) who were littering the stage. On the first night I caught my foot in the flex of a heavy lamp and, in an attempt to stay upright, ran straight out the other side. Each performance ended in uproar; and at the end of the week Anton Dolin himself issued a statement to the effect that never again would the Festival Ballet make use of cheap undergraduate labour. Clearly if we were to make progress, we would do better to sing than to dance.

In our third year we moved into digs in St John Street and lived the life of Riley. We danced to Tommy Kinsman, and drove down to the station to meet the 'fornication flyer' which brought girls up from London promptly by steam in time to change at the Mitre or the Randolph. Once, I remember, Michael was let down by some girl: he advertised for a partner in *Isis* and took his pick of the applicants. It was a golden summer, or so it now seems from the perspective of thirty years, with the limestone spires of the city touched by the rays of the setting sun.

I came down from Oxford in 1954. I was faced with the problem of how to make a living — I married Paula Baron in the following year — and the necessity of winning a place upon the 'candidate's list' of political aspirants, kept by Central Office: without inclusion I could never stand for Parliament, at least in the Conservative interest. I wanted to write for the newspapers and to that end I was interviewed by Colin Coote at the *Daily Telegraph*. He held out no hope of a job in Fleet Street but did offer a two year stint on a paper in Wigan as a proper preparation. Neither Paula nor I could face so daunting an exile, so I followed her advice and went into advertising as an executive trainee with Lintas, the Unilever advertising agency. I was not much of an executive, but would have done well writing copy, but my salary and hers (she was a visualiser with Masius and Fergusson) kept the wolf at bay. Married at Caxton Hall, working in Portman Square, all that remained was to win the Party's stamp of approval.

Harold Macmillan once said that the only quality necessary for a Member of Parliament was the ability to write a good letter. But times have changed. The Conservative Party has adopted all the techniques of the 'head-hunter' in its search for and scrutiny of its future MPs. An MP is appointed a Vice-Chairman of the party organisation with the sole responsibility of picking and choosing, and the mesh has been woven fine indeed. References are taken up and, what is worse, the party subjects the ambitious to a weekend at a Berkshire motel, where, for a fee of forty pounds, they are put through their paces before a panel of MPs, industrialists and party big-wigs. The aspirant is called upon to lead a discussion, write a paper, be interviewed 'in depth', conduct an interview and take part in a debate. He is put under stress and his performance closely observed. He is forced to jump through intellectual hoops and marked up, or down, on his table manners.

I was recently invited to attend this ordeal as an observer. Forty-eight men and women, some black but overwhelmingly white and middle class, began their examination by sitting in a circle, numbered fore and aft, discussing whether we have the press we deserve, and the effect of high rewards upon the behaviour of tennis players. After a desultory discussion, a group task was set. One such group were told that in just under four weeks' time they were to attend a candidate's selection committee in a Conservative-held marginal seat. How should the group brief itself about local conditions so that the best impression is made? The group must pick a spokesman. His response could be paraphrased as spending time beforehand with the editor of the local newspaper — exactly the advice that Philip Goodhart gave me when I was seeking adoption in Aldershot.

Next, a thousand word essay was to be completed in two hours on the subject of youth unemployment. While they scribbled they were summoned one by one to an interview conducted by an MP (in this case Chris Patten) which lasts for half an hour, followed by yet another interview with the Chief Assessor. The evening ended with a formal dinner, duck and green peas, but no toasts or speeches. Next morning the groups had to reach an agreed conclusion on the topic on which they had written their essays. This was followed by an interview in which one candidate offered three non-political subjects of his choice and was then interviewed by another on one of them. The topics included playing the organ, fox hunting and opera. The final exercise was a debate. The subject was announced, in this case censorship, and half an hour allocated to preparing a case and picking two 'front bench' speakers. The two groups then debated the one against the other in an ideal but unrealisable Parliamentary situation in which every backbencher gets called.

After a light lunch the Chief Assessor, the MP, the Group Leader and a visiting industrialist representing the real world, met to compare notes, harmonise their impressions and build up a final mark sheet. Candidates are graded into one of five possible positions: strong, good, adequate, limited and weak. The sheet itself is divided into three: the candidate's intellectual potential; practical potential; and character and personality potential. Anything from adequate downwards is failed or at least deferred. The conclusions are then vetted by Central Office. The failure rate is 23%.

Is it all worthwhile? The good and the bad pick themselves; where it is useful is in grading the greys, those who ought either to be discouraged or encouraged. The process was entirely lacking in ideological content — 'wets' were not discriminated against — and carried out with great care and scrupulous fairness. In the past the party relied upon the most able of the middle class to be the yeast in an aristocratic leaven (e.g. the 1950 intake). Gentlemen went into politics as an extension of their social obligation. Today, the Tory Party is overwhelmingly bourgeois. Yet filtration is good only as far as it goes; it cannot solve the real problem, which is how to attract the best into politics. Central Office is beginning to rely upon 'the touch on the shoulder', the invitation to people of obvious talent to come into politics. One such invitee, who was the star of the Berkshire bunch, was Virginia Bottomley who held S. W. Surrey in the by-election early in 1984. She was selected, beating Ian Sproat, a former Minister, and Stanley Johnson, a MEP, to become the party's candidate, but the selection took place behind closed doors. My attempt to persuade Mr Peter Brewer, the Chairman of the Association, to open up the final to press and television, failed. It would have been 'unfair to the participants'. I disagree.

All this was in vivid contrast to what happened in the fifties. I was interviewed by a nice old buffer who once he had checked up on my schooling (Shrewsbury, the Sorbonne and Oxford) told me that he had been a friend of my father's. I thought it unlikely but said nothing. He had known him well both at Imperial Airways and on the links; he thought the world of Diana; but did not care overmuch for greyhound racing. I murmured some protest but he was quite remorseless. 'One of the best,' he said, 'remember him in the House.' He was referring, of course, to Brigadier Critchley, 'Critch' of pre-war fame, a Canadian adventurer who had been for a time a Beaverbrook-sponsored MP. It was not to be the last time the mistake was made. We chatted for a time; I told him that, once elected, I would specialise in agriculture and foreign affairs, which was, after all, only estate management on a larger scale. He looked pleased and showed me to the door. In a week's time I had a letter welcoming me to the list.

I was lucky to be adopted for Rochester and Chatham at my first attempt. Arthur Bottomley had won the seat for Labour after the war from a Captain Plugge, who had started Radio Luxembourg and was remembered by the local Tories for his lavish parties at the Dorchester whither they had been carried by charabanc. A John Campbell had tried and failed to win the seat back in '50, while Robert Mathew had been no more fortunate in '51 and '55: despite everything, 'Arthur' had held on, increasing his majority each time. Perhaps the local committee had secretly despaired, for I had little to offer save youth and the vigour which should accompany it. Anyway, I was picked, and for two years I drove down the A2 from Blackheath, where we were living, to what seemed an endless round of canvassing, ward meetings, wine and cheese and infrequently held and ill attended public meetings. At long last in 1959 Harold Macmillan called a general election for October 15. I was ready to do or die.

At Rochester during the election we were visited by the great. A crucial marginal, in the jargon of the trade, we had to win if the party were to take up once again its rightful place at the helm of the Nation's affairs . . . the rhetoric is catching. 'Super Mac' himself passed through the Medway Towns by motorcar, and for a mile or two I was permitted to sit next to him, not daring to speak. 'Beastly things, elections,' he murmured, and bared his teeth.

Charles Hill spoke at the Chatham Town Hall; twenty minutes of beef stew, served up in a rich gravy, demotic, funny and delivered with a marvellous self-confidence that turned every interruption to his advantage. He was, in his prime, the best platform speaker in the party, less cerebral than Quintin Hogg, more assured with the public than Harold Macmillan, less distant than Rab Butler. Macleod came down later to speak to a club of Tory businessmen, but he was never at his best keeping the wheels of Rotary turning. After it was over we drove back to London. 'I thought my lot were dreadful till I met yours,' was his only comment. Sir Alfred Bossom, once MP for Maidstone and a survivor from before the war, was drafted in as President for the local party: he took the chair at the meetings.

At Rochester, at the culmination of four weeks hard, came surprise victory, a two thousand Labour majority overturned and replaced by one of 1013. We did not go to bed that October night. I had made it, and against the odds. Whatever the future, it was, as Trollope wrote, no mean thing to have the initials MP after your name.

3   The Macmillan Years

In October '59, when I first drove into New Palace Yard in my brand new Ford Popular, there was still something of 'Chips' Channon about the Tory Party. Today, the Tory Party in the House contains the Party Conference of ten years ago. Cheerful girls in hats who once moved conference motions in favour of corporal and capital punishment on behalf of the Young Conservatives of some Midlands town, small town solicitors and estate agents with flat, provincial accents, are now its Members. As Mrs Thatcher has gone up in the world, so the party has come down.

Twenty years ago you could tell a Tory just by looking at him. He was well suited. The party still retained something of its pre-war sleekness; elderly gentlemen in Trumper's haircuts, wearing cream silk shirts and Brigade or Old Etonian ties. Everyone seemed related to everyone else. I was for ever being accosted, when sitting quietly in the Smoking Room (the far corner of which was occasionally occupied by the grander Labour MP such as Hugh Gaitskell or Richard Crossman), by nice old buffers who claimed to have known my father. Many had had 'a good war', and one cure for contempt was to discover, while sitting in the Library during all night sittings, a slim volume such as *How I Rowed across the North Sea Singlehanded* by Sir Hugh Monroe Lucas-Tooth.

Within my first week or so in the House, I was sitting in the Smoking Room reading a book. Charles Hill, who had spoken for me at the Chatham Town Hall during the election, came up to me. 'Young man, it does not do to appear clever: advancement in this man's party is due entirely to alcoholic stupidity.' I have taken care never to open a book since.

If the Tory Party had had a good war, it was not so happy about the peace. Mr Harold Macmillan, that 'nice ass', according to 'Chips', who complained in his diary that Macmillan feared a Labour win in 1945, was believed by many on the back benches to be leading the party in directions that were uncongenial. When all was said, had not Macmillan sat on the back benches for twenty years before the war, regarded by the Whips' Office of the day — truly a confederacy of dunces — as 'unsound'? As Churchill once said to Macmillan, 'Had it not been for Hitler neither of us would be where he is today.'

I sat uneasily in this assembly of bumblebees. Shrewsbury, the Sorbonne and Pembroke College, Oxford, enabled me, or so I thought, to pass for white, although of my grandfathers, one had been a railwayman on the London and North Western and the other a clerk in Bristol Gas Works. I gave up the stiff white collars that I had worn at the advertising agency and was careful to wear plain ties; but my suits were Burton's at £10 a time. One evening I was in the 'No' lobby waiting to file past the clerks to record my vote on a three-line whip. Out of a crowd of more than three hundred I noticed Sir Jocelyn Lucas, with whom I had never exchanged a word, making his way determinedly in my direction, and I watched him breast the wave like Captain Webb, twisting and turning. Could he be about to invite me to dinner? Or to congratulate me on my maiden speech? He took my elbow in the palm of his hand. 'You're wearin' suede shoes,' he said, and promptly vanished. Today we are all wearing suede shoes.

Seventy-one Conservatives were first elected to Parliament in October 1959, an election which, until Mrs Thatcher's triumph in June '83, marked the high tide in the party's fortunes. The 'fifty-niners' were once described by R. A. Butler, then at the height of his powers, as 'the poorest intake in my experience'. Were we that bad? Butler was making a comparison with the famous 1950 intake, a vintage year, and we were plainly not so glittering. Even so, we can claim one Prime Minister, Mrs Thatcher, about whom the last word has not yet been written, and Mr James Prior, long regarded by the more moderate Conservative as the acceptable face of Toryism. After that we do begin to fall away somewhat: nevertheless, the 'fifty-niners' included Peter Tapsell, who has preferred the City to Westminster, and who might be described, without hyperbole, as the most able Tory never to have been given office. Nicholas Ridley, an elegant monetarist, is in the Cabinet, having been rescued by the arrival of Mrs Thatcher, while Sir Geoffrey Johnson Smith has been a Minister and a Vice-Chairman of the party in charge of candidate selection. Perhaps the most interesting of the '59 vintage are the two who did not stay the course; Christopher Chataway and Humphry Berkeley. In 1959, Chris Chataway appeared to be the most promising of the new intake. A world class athlete, a telly personality and responsible, with other Bow Groupers, for the setting up of World Refugee Year, he was stamped from the mould of the clever and concerned Conservative, a follower of Macmillan, Butler and Macleod, conventional but able, and it was not many months before he was promoted to the obscurity of junior office.

Humphry Berkeley was more radical. No respecter of persons, however stuffed, he can lay claim to having been the most influential Tory backbencher since the war. Responsible in large part for homosexual law reform, and in small for the abolition of capital punishment, his most significant achievement was to lead the campaign that led to the change in the way in which the Conservative Party picked its leader, substituting election by the 1922 Committee for the 'emergence' through the taking of soundings which had been responsible for the elevation of Sir Alec Douglas-Home. It was to prove a mixed blessing. But Berkeley lost his seat and patience with the party, moving first to Labour and then to the Social Democrats. Chataway quit politics in '74 in favour of merchant banking. How comfortable he would have felt in today's Tory Party is a matter for conjecture, but it is likely that he would have featured in at least the first of Mrs Thatcher's Cabinets.

The other member of the '59 intake to be promoted from the back benches during that Parliament was Margaret Thatcher. I had little to do with her and can remember little save for a lunch at which she shared a table with Peter Kirk, David Walder and myself. She must have made an impression of sorts; I can distinctly recall David Walder saying of her afterwards that she reminded him of the Chairman of his Women's Advisory Committee 'writ hideously large'. Mrs Thatcher's fundamentalism — she seemed not simply to reflect but to amplify the views of her constituents — was at that time deeply unfashionable. On the back benches in the early sixties, the moderate Tories sought change, such as decolonialisation, and the party's ballast, continuity: today all has changed; the ballast seeks change, an end to the politics of consensus, and the moderates or 'wets', so called, continuity.

In the sixties, under the leadership of Harold Macmillan, the party was moderate, even progressive, in tone; its stance having been taken from Churchill (a Liberal-Imperialist?), and those of his supporters who came to power with him in 1940. The exception was the one-time Chamberlainite 'Rab' Butler, whose contribution in persuading the Conservative party to adopt and pursue the social and economic policies of the Grand Coalition of the war, was second to no one. But the Knights of the Shires clearly preferred Burke's *Peerage* to Burke's *Reflections*, and their successors, the Knights of the Suburbs, have gone on doing so to this day. The old Adam has given way to the new Eve.

And what of the great? The '59 Parliament saw the decline and fall of Harold Macmillan, who had in '57 come to the aid of a demoralised Government and party, a party which he had led to victory two years later with a majority of a hundred seats. On my arrival, elected to Westminster on his coat tails, he bestrode the world with his carefully cultivated elegance and wit, imperturbable at Prime Minister's Questions and on the great occasion, betraying his anxiety when addressing the 1922 Committee by the nervousness with which he fingered his Brigade tie. He knew he was not among friends.

A month after the election, Peter Emery, one of the newcomers, arranged a dinner at the East India Club for the newly elected at which the Prime Minister spoke. Some of us literally sat at the Great Man's feet. The effect of Harold Macmillan's charm is legendary, and it is at its most potent when directed towards the young. 'Revolt by all means, ' he told us, 'but only on one issue at a time; to do more is to confuse the Whips.' He talked of Stockton and of unemployment before the war. He warned us not to become impatient with the 'Majors' in our party: 'Every regiment has its Majors.' He spoke of his desire above all else to prevent the outbreak of a Third World War.

I was hooked. Here at last was someone on whose behalf I could unsheathe my sword, such as it was. Later I wrote his obituary for *The Times*, inheriting one that had been written by Sir William Haley. It began, 'This man has been a national disaster . .' I tore it up and began again. What is more I stayed loyal. At the height of the 'Profumo Affair', which was gleefully used by his enemies in the party, the *Guardian* reported a speech I had made to the Hampstead Young Conservatives:'"Prime Minister must not be brought down by two tarts," says Tory back bencher.' Unfortunately, he was.

For the most part, however, I sat a spectator throughout the noise and nonsense of the 'Profumo Affair'. What can now be said is that George Wigg undoubtedly set out, with malice aforethought, to destroy Profumo for reasons which were as much personal as political. Wigg was cantankerous and self-important, a former sergeant-major, whose knowledge of the minutiae of defence policy enabled him to play the part of gad-fly. He seized upon Profumo's peccadillos with glee, although not always with accuracy. I can remember him telling me, as we stood together in the gents, that he had discovered that the Secretary for War was 'a massive homosexual'. This comment, which could hardly, in retrospect, have been more fatuous, was made to me some months before the scandal broke. 'Profumo' was to colour an affair in which the English demonstrated their prurience, the newspapers their hypocrisy, and our Whips' Office, its monumental incompetence. The chief victim was not John Profumo, it was the Prime Minister.

I was lucky enough to hear Aneurin Bevan's last speech — he was to die of cancer a few months later — on the debate on the Address. He spoke from the despatch box, facing a Government side packed to the rafters with the newly elected. He gently ribbed us: 'What is the prospect before you?' he asked. 'I will tell you. It is hours and hours of infinite boredom.' He was right.

To someone of twenty-eight, the House seemed full of Titans. Winston Churchill, locked into silence by the hardness of his cerebral arteries, never spoke, but sat broodingly in his place, a wheelchair awaiting his departure in the Members' Lobby. After questions he would be taken to the Smoking Room where he would sit while the Whips drummed up Members to come and sit with him. Greatly alarmed, I was pressed into service. I asked him whether he would like a cup of tea. He fixed me with a watery, pale blue eye and replied, 'No, you bloody fool, a double whisky.' I happily obliged.

Twenty years ago the Chamber was better attended and the speech in the House remained the best method of self-promotion. Today we can write articles, appear on television, sometimes on our own programmes, write books and pamphlets and perform on Select Committees; in consequence the Chamber is poorly attended by a handful of Members who wait impatiently to be called and having spoken, quit the Chamber for refreshment. The wind-up, in particular, has suffered. In the sixties the House would fill up at nine o'clock at the end of a major debate, confident as to the quality of the entertainment. The Government's case would be made by one of a trio of superb performers: Charles Hill, who was robust and funny, Peter Thorneycroft, whose bulk had bent a thousand platforms, and John Boyd Carpenter, who was never shouted down. Whatever the merit of the case, in those days we never sweated at the palms. Then as now the Opposition front bench below the gangway was the home of the awkward squad, but who can compare the subtle challenge of Sidney Silverman, a clever barrack room lawyer whose duel of wits with the Speaker, Sir Harry Hylton Foster, held the House enthralled, something which is much to be preferred to the Public Bar abuse which is the stock in trade of the rougher end of the Labour Party.

I found it all rather alarming. It was easier to win public attention by the propagation of unorthodox views outside the Chamber, and a glance at my scrapbooks of the period — for in those days I was vain enough to subscribe to a press cuttings service — reveals just how much coverage I received. I wanted to become a defence expert and as a first step to becoming one, I read Alastair Buchan's *Nato in the Sixties*, an intelligent critique of traditional defence policies. My maiden speech was an attack on Government policy. I wrote a pamphlet for the Bow Group questioning what I saw to be an undue reliance on the part of Britain and the West on nuclear weapons. I teamed up with Nigel Birch, Anthony Head and Fitzroy Maclean to attack the Government's decision to abolish National Service. The press picked me out as 'a coming man' whose views were much in advance of those of the Government, let alone the bulk of my colleagues on the back benches. I was in favour of 'Britain in Europe', urged swifter decolonialisation and was more Macleodite than Iain Macleod, though not half as clever. In short, I was a pain in the party's neck.

How severe a pain I was to learn in 1961, a year in which I began to write a regular 'Westminster Commentary' for Brian Inglis's *Spectator*. Bernard Braine, who was a junior Health Minister and who had met and admired my father at a meeting of the General Medical Council, asked me if I would like to be his Parliamentary Private Secretary. I was only too delighted, for to be a PPS was to put a first step on the rungs of the ladder. But it was not to be. A day or so later I was summoned to the Whips' Office by the Deputy Chief Whip, Michael Hughes Young and told there was no question of my becoming a PPS. 'The party would not wear it,' he said. This was the only explanation ever offered.

I was soon to be in even hotter water. Michael Heseltine, who was at that time a close friend and not yet in the House, asked me whether I would like a suit. As my mother-in-law had recently been told at a dinner party by Sir William Teeling that I was probably the worst-dressed Member of Parliament, I accepted Michael's kind offer. The suggestion was that I should be photographed in a suit especially designed for an MP, to appear in a feature to be carried by *Town* magazine, a glossy published by Michael Heseltine and Clive Labovitch, which would include a suit for a doctor, lawyer etc. I was duly measured and photographed by some trendy working-class photographer. A month or so later *Town* appeared with my photograph in it. I must admit I was rather appalled. And so were others.

In my absence the affair was raised at the weekly meeting of the 1922 Committee. 'The fella's modellin', Major

Morrison.' I was once again summoned to the Whips' Office, this time by the Chief Whip, Martin Redmayne, who was to end his days working at Harrods. I was not asked to sit down. A copy of *Town* lay upon his otherwise empty desk. Redmayne picked it up between finger and thumb and asked, 'Are ye hard up?' I said I wasn't. Had I admitted to being so I might well have been paid a monthly remittance from party funds, providing I lived in Alice Springs. The suit, which was black and pompous, with a white waistcoat lasted me for years, but it was no substitute for promotion.

To have been in politics and not tasted office must be rather like a soldier in war who has never heard a shot fired in anger. But there is something to be said for life behind the lines. Junior Ministers are chauffeur-driven into obscurity, reappearing once a month at question time in order to read out replies prepared beforehand by some Wykehamist. Occasionally they reply to an adjournment debate held in the small hours. They are excluded from the weekly meetings of the 1922 Committee, that theatre of the absurd which is the political equivalent of an ENSA concert party. Frankly, I doubt if I could have endured four years as Parliamentary Secretary to the Department of Health and Social Security stuck in some slum at the Elephant and Castle, actually answering my own constituency letters.

I was attracted to office but have talked myself out of it. I was never persuaded to take the necessary vows of poverty, chastity and obedience, although I would have been tempted in my extreme youth by the offer of a short spell in the Whips' Office, that cheerful freemasonry where I might have learnt to distinguish between those of my colleagues who had 'bottom', whatever that means, and those who had not. It is not really possible to understand the nature of that complex and subtle animal the Conservative Party without having been a member of the Broederbund.

Life at Westminster, I was soon to discover, has its risks. I was told very early on by an elderly Knight of the Shire who looked like Harold Macmillan and bred Sealyhams, that the two occupational hazards of life at Westminster were alcohol and adultery. 'The Lords,' he said severely, 'has the cup for adultery.' I have been attracted to both although middle life and the misfortunes of others have served to blunt my appetite. The haroosh that follows the intermittent revelation of the sexual goings-on of an unlucky MP has convinced me that the only safe pleasure for a parliamentarian is a bag of boiled sweets. The alternative, as many have learnt to their cost, leads to the ultimate humiliation — being pilloried on moral grounds by our popular press.

Alcohol can improve the quality of front bench speeches, but not by very much. It can help, too, when the House suspends the ten o'clock rule and business continues into the watches of the night. But its consumption does tend to encourage those MPs of all parties who can neither speak with effect nor be silent with dignity.

But what are the compensations for a life spent scrutinising

the backs of the heads of members of one's own party for signs of intelligence? The best that can be extracted from a life high up on the Government back benches can only be the ringside seat at great events. Any first year undergraduate will tell you that power has gone from the MP first into the executive, from Government into the bureaucracy and from the bureaucracy into the institutions. The backbench member of the Government party has but one task, and that is to sustain the Government in office. He is courted by the Whips not for his voice but for his vote. He is a privileged spectator with limited access to the media. In the early sixties he was poorly paid (£1750 a year), today he is still comparatively poorly paid (£17,000) but his salary is buttressed by generous car, secretarial, research and living expenses. But most MPs earn as much again outside. As October 1964 approached and with it the date of the general election, I knew deep down that I would lose my seat. On the day of dissolution I made a silent tour of the building, determined to return one day for some seat or another. I had made a modest name as a Tory rebel and a lot of friends. And I had enjoyed myself hugely.

4   The Lowest Form of Political Life

'The earnest party man becomes a silent drudge, tramping at intervals through the lobbies to record his vote and wondering why he comes to Westminster at all.'

Winston Churchill

I have never been an earnest party man. I have tramped regularly through the lobbies to record my vote, which is almost invariably cast in favour of the Government (or Tory Opposition), and there have been many times when I have wondered whether or not I have been wasting my time. Should I not have given it all up and gone out and done a proper job? I might have gone to California as a butler in some lovely home, my task to take red wine out of fridges, or to work at London Airport, the only white man to drive a courtesy bus. Jim Wellbeloved, the Labour MP who joined the SDP, was once reported to have said that membership of the House of Commons was 'better than working', and he has a point.

To succeed in politics the politician needs the religious temperament, capable of faith without scrutiny. He must eschew doubt. The man on the make must put his party on a pedestal and himself in hock. At best he can rise to high office; at the worst he can live a life of indolence, winning commendation by saying nothing, even listening to nothing, but simply voting in the right lobby when the Whips require it. He has a quiet life and his local party, which is usually unaware of the extent or otherwise of his extra-constituency activities, is perfectly satisfied.

The party system serves to stifle MPs, but is not entirely without advantage. Membership of the political party of one's choice can provide the ticket without which a journey

39

to Westminster is, in today's political climate, impossible. The 'package' includes a range of policies, behind which a MP can shelter, calling in aid to the disenchanted that a matter of controversy is party policy. The manifesto, even among Conservatives, has begun to take on something of the quality of Holy Writ. The Free Vote, which is used sparingly in order to rid the political parties of unnecessary difficulty on subjects of 'conscience' (a nice-mindedness which is not supposed to apply to more mundane matters) is permitted for subjects such as abortion and the restoration of capital punishment. Even fluoridisation has been liberated in this manner.

The Free Vote is not always made welcome. It leaves the backbencher unprotected, at the mercy either of nuns or *Guardian* women on abortion, the former, if there are many Catholics in the constituency, being the more powerful lobby. Harold Macmillan once said that if the people want a moral lead they should go to their Bishops, a point of view which Mrs Thatcher would not share. On abortion, I take the view that it is a regrettable necessity, a view which is probably shared by the majority of my electors. But they do not march on Westminster.

The restoration of capital punishment is also left to a Free Vote. The Tories divide two thirds/one third in favour, and it is judged best by the party managers to leave MPs to their own devices. Aldershot has suffered from IRA bomb outrages, such as the attack in 1972 on a Parachute Regiment barracks which killed seven, and from several horrific murders. My abolitionist stance has, therefore, not been popular. If members of the IRA will starve themselves to death in order to make a political point, execution at the hands of the 'Brits' would clearly be doing them a favour: as for murder, plain and simple, I would like to think that society can still do without the death penalty, given the probability of eventual error.

My passion in politics was for Europe. In the early sixties it appealed to my idealism: it was, and still is, a cause for which I could draw my sword. I was converted to 'the European ideal' by Roy Jenkins, who, at that time, spoke both within and beyond the House of Commons with an enthusiasm which I found beguiling. It was a cause which

Harold Macmillan embraced, and which Ted Heath consummated: it has been left to others to neglect it.

My wish to see Britain eventually merge its sovereignty into a United States of Europe, while keeping its identity and throne, is unlikely to be realised. The retailers, in a wholesale world, have taken charge. I have never had much patience with those who seem, by their stridency, to equate 'sovereignty' with 'virginity': once lost, neither is worth regaining. A united Europe, secure in its own defence, would have the power and the population to regain its independence as a super power in its own right. The ancient nation states of Europe are the cradle of our civilisation; how tiresome it is that we are still obliged to celebrate victories in what should be, by now, regarded as civil wars. By repute a cynic, I am no Nationalist, and my 'cynicism' is probably a pose designed to compensate for a frustrated romanticism. If my admiration for Mrs Thatcher is somewhat qualified, it is because she has continually demanded the price of everything while remaining ignorant of its value.

I went into politics to seek fame; I have yet to find it. Fame is the spur. Anyone in public life who tells you differently is not telling the truth. I have never made the front bench, although I have spoken from it on several occasions in Opposition, by virtue of my chairmanship of the Media and Defence Committees. Has then my sole task as a backbencher been simply to sustain a Conservative Government in office? I fear so. What have been the limits to my freedom, and are those limits to be found in the Whips' Office or in the impatience of my constituency party, whether in Rochester or Aldershot?

It is not for me to say why it is I have stayed on the back benches for twenty years. One reason may be a tendency to irreverence, a perverse proclivity to argue the toss. I have been inclined to rummage among the tablets of stone. In the eighties I went to have a drink in Wilton Street with Edward Heath and he said to me, 'I have never understood why a man as clever and able as you has never set out to dominate the House of Commons.' Taken aback, I could only mumble something about a lack of self-confidence. But the implication of his somewhat typically blunt remark was pleasingly flattering.

But mute and inglorious, I have at least enjoyed myself. It is tempting for the backbencher to behave as if he were a Congressman, with a fief of his own, operating independently within a system in which the political parties are much weaker than in fact they are. The truth is, of course, that the Executive has handed back to the political parties, which, to be fair, provided the ladder up which I climbed into Westminster, the power which it has wrested from Parliament itself.

The ambitious backbencher (and, as Henry Fairlie has claimed, 'ambition is the engine of the public good') must live on hope — hope that he will be swiftly recognised and that he will be considered not only able but 'sound', which suggesting as it does a willingness to go down with the ship, is the highest term of praise employed by the Conservative Whips, and not a 'shit', which is the somewhat inelegant label bestowed by the Whips on those they consider tiresome.

The term 'shit' demands an explanation. As a comment by Whip upon Member, it is more than just a vulgar word of abuse. It has overtones of class; it is clubby and regimental. It is the contempt of one officer for another, or of Eton for Harrow. It is also double-barrelled, for at one level it suggests that an MP so described is rebellious and therefore unreliable ('the fella's forever rockin' the boat'), at another it hints at some weakness of character such as malice, indiscretion or disloyalty; thus if you are not winged by one barrel, you will be by the other. What the Whips look for is reliability linked to ability. Expertise is unnecessary, even dangerous — what are civil servants for? There will never be a shortage of advice; the task of the politicians is to choose. Clement Attlee is supposed to have advised the young Roy Mason to 'specialise and stay out of the bars.' No Tory would ever have given such advice.

It is in such a way that the milk is skimmed. The backbencher does have one function, however, which I believe to be of great importance: he should moderate the views of his supporters. He must help to sustain the Government in office, and he is expected, when in Opposition, to make out the worst possible case for the Government's actions but he has not been sent to Westminster to blow other men's trumpets. The party activist has a tendency to hanker after the unobtainable and to see the complexities of politics in black and white; the MP is not the creature of some unrepresentative and self-selected Management or Executive Committee but, *vide* Burke, the representative in Parliament of the constituency as a whole. Only by standing up against the views of the extremist can social and political cohesion be maintained, a lesson which we are in great danger of forgetting.

The relationship that most matters in a politician's life is the one between him and his constituency party, for it has the power of adoption and readoption; to stand for Parliament without a party label of any kind is to court disaster. Independents do not get elected, so dominant have party politics become since the war. A Conservative candidate will have been chosen by the Executive Committee of the local association from a list of names of candidates-to-be, submitted by Central Office. Two hundred or so, the most active of the 'activists', will make the choice, a minute proportion of those who will vote for the candidate at the election. Party activists, who are believed to number less than 2% of the population, are thus an unrepresentative minority (in that they care about politics).

In the Tory Party the party worker is inclined to buttress his loyalty to the party by support for whatever might be the prevailing fashion: for example under Heath most activists were in favour of entry into Europe; under Margaret the majority support her economic policies. As a body they certainly have no objection to political truisms, emphatically delivered, as can be seen at the annual Party Conference. When a Conservative Government is unpopular they tend to shrink in number, the residue frequently becoming more extreme.

To the layman whose political activity consists of grumbling interspersed with the infrequent casting of a vote, 'Tory women', or the image of them which is presented by press and television, conjures up pictures of tweedy women with cut-glass voices towed by Labradors, comfortable middle-aged bodies in unspeakable hats who sit quietly knitting through the rowdiest of debates and cheerful girls brandishing handcuffs at the rostrum. But, in truth, such

43

snapshots, like quotations from a speech, can tell us less than half the story. Most of the Tory women I have known would not hurt a fly.

And I should know. For twenty years I have been lunching badly with them, tramping mean streets in their company, holding my torch in frozen fingers so that they can mark up on their canvas cards the prejudices of the electors upon whom they have just called. I have danced with them, young and old, enveloped in clouds of blue tulle and sipped as many cups of milky Nescafé as would stretch from Smith Square to the Metropole Hotel, Brighton.

The 'Tory woman' is most in evidence at the annual Party Conference where, at a seaside resort out of season, several thousand of them take shelter from the autumnal gales inside Winter Gardens in order to be flattered, cajoled and exhorted by the members of Mrs Thatcher's Cabinet, performances which, regardless of quality, are invariably rewarded by a standing ovation.

It is, I suppose, as 'hangers and floggers', stridently demanding the return of rod and rope, that 'Tory women' are thought to come into their own. But, to be fair, it is a subject about which many women can be expected to feel frightened and vulnerable. The inevitable debate on crime and punishment always presents the platform with its most exacting task, a test which has in the past been overcome by such consummate conjurors and sleight-of-hand artists as 'Rab' Butler and Willie Whitelaw. The fact that if there is an 'answer' to rising crime then it lies in the certainty of conviction rather than the intensity of punishment is not one which it is easy to put across to an emotionally charged mass meeting.

But all is soon forgiven. On the final day of the jamboree, Mrs Thatcher herself, proof, as if it were needed, of the proposition that women are the stronger sex, addresses the Conference, the faces of her assembled Cabinet turned avidly in her direction. As she declaims each carefully constructed (and endlessly reconstructed) paragraph, her audience, a large majority of which consists of women, goes through the necessary process of the recharging of batteries, new power that will enable them to face the tedium, aggravation and, to be frank, pleasure of yet another year spent on the stump.

In Aldershot the local Conservative Association is run by women. Most of our activities, conferences, supper clubs, lunchtime meetings and the annual dinner and dance would not take place were it not for the hard work of the women. They man the committee rooms, tell outside polling stations, address envelopes, and, most important of all, raise the money. But rarely do they talk politics. Personalities, yes; but policies, infrequently.

Yet the activities of the constituency parties, however mundane they may seem, are part of a continuous process of creating mutual confidence, evolving local leaders and impressing outsiders by the assumption of success. The local Tory Association does provide a platform, the help of an agent and staff and a network of friendship upon which the MP must rely. The Conservative Party has not yet been put into uniform, is more moderate and accommodating than is Labour, as has been shown all too clearly by the adoption of a nationwide process of candidate reselection. We believe in the parson's freehold. The Conservative Party is still in some ways the non-political political party, something which gives a degree of freedom to its MPs. But I should make two provisos: as I have already said, in the Tory party it is much more difficult to break to the left; and, in the last analysis, there are clearly limits beyond which the MP should not go, for it will be the candidate's job to carry the party's standard into battle at the next election.

Belloc and Chesterton both believed that the party caucus had replaced the whole body of the electors as the main menace to the Member's integrity, and whereas this may have been true in the past, and Nigel Nicolson's dispute in Bournemouth East, over Suez, in particular, comes to mind, I have never found it to have been the case, despite having tried from time to time the patience of my local party. While attempting to represent my constituency, in the sense that it is my duty to bring its grievances to the attention of Parliament, I have remained my own man. I owe my party my allegiance, but I have never undertaken to follow blindly the vagaries of its leaders or its policies.

For the MP, stranded by the receding tide of ambition upon the back benches, there are choices to be made. He can get out. He can pursue politics with voice and pen, using the media to project his personality and opinion, an activity which may bring him pleasure, profit, prominence and some influence upon events — Lord Boothby remains the classic example of the major minor figure. He can, however, sink into a torpor of acquiescence, for being an MP is rather like being a parson in the Church of England — you can do as much or as little as you like. This can be rewarded either by a knighthood, or by a peerage, a ticket to the Lords, that 'sunset home' where the company is congenial and the food good (bread and butter pudding served by aged retainers) and the power of party less evident. Or he can concentrate upon the bar, or upon business. Whatever his choice, no obstacle is raised, for what the Whips require of him is his vote, not his voice.

After my defeat by a thousand votes at Rochester I wrote that my motives for going into politics were two: service and ambition. Twenty years later it is not for me to say which has played the greater part. But I had enjoyed a ringside seat and I was determined to regain it.

While I was in the House I joined the Bow Group of young Tories which was beginning to make a name for itself. The YCs were the foot-soldiers of the party, their task to tramp the streets, canvas cards in hand, identifying friend and foe; they were not for me. The Bow Group, on the other hand, had acquired a reputation for brains: several young men of a studious bent, who were later to become famous — Geoffrey Howe, Patrick Jenkin, David Howell and David Windlesham — were assiduous scribblers of party tracts, the guts of which were extracted by a hungry press. I found the headline 'Bow Groupers challenge Government' an exciting one, and I was eager to take part.

The Bow Group is the most distinguished of the 'outside' Tory groupings, that is bodies which attract MPs and others. The Monday Club, originally a group of the old, traditional right of the party, has slid recently into obscurity by way of the more discreditable aspects of our party, such as racialism. Within the House of Commons is found its more respectable counterpart, the Club of 92, the child of Major Sir Patrick Wall, a nice old cold war warrior. He has been replaced by Mr George Gardiner, the MP for Reigate.

The Club of 92, the purpose of which was to keep the party firmly to the right (at which it has clearly succeeded), has one advantage over its rivals; it is permitted to recruit not only from back benchers but from Ministers, senior and junior, a privilege denied to others. Mr Norman Tebbit has been heard to remark of the Club of 92 that it carries 'no taint of intellectualism', which does not come as a surprise. Sir William Clark, known as 'the Rotarian General', serves as its figurehead. The Club is at its busiest at the time of the annual elections to party committees, when it helps to run the campaign for its members.

The Club of 92 is matched by the Lollards, named after the Lollards Tower in Lambeth Palace under the eaves of which lives Mr William van Straubenzee, a stout 'wet'. He, too, has given way; in this case to Mr Fred Sylvester, who with the help of his adjutant, Colonel Mates, plots to have more moderate Tories elected to committee office.

The newly-elected tend to huddle together for comfort. In the 1979 Parliament the Blue Chips, a band of the more gilded 'wets', Mr William Waldegrave, Mr Chris Patten, Mr Garel Jones, met secretly to worry, over indifferent claret, about the progress of Mrs Thatcher's counter-revolution. They were promptly rewarded by junior office, and have disappeared from view.

The most prestigious of these 'inside' groups is the One Nation, formed in the fifties, its purpose being to remind the party of its Disraelian inheritance. MPs quit on receiving office, and are, sometimes, invited to rejoin years later. Its Chairman is Mr William Benyon, and it includes the more talented back benchers such as Mr Douglas Hogg and Mr Nigel Foreman. It dines on Wednesdays, and is, despite Sir Philip Goodhart's recently published pamphlet, *Jobs Ahead*, a plea for more employment, perhaps not quite the force it was twenty years ago. But it does still attract a better class of person.

Other bodies such as the Number Five Group, which meets to listen to Mr George Walden, and the Third Term Group, come and go as events and people dictate. The Club of 92 provides the foot soldiers of the right; its officers are more likely to be members of the Conservative Philosophy Group to which congenial outsiders are sometimes invited. It is a club for Fogeys, young and old, clever young men wearing their fathers' suits but who, at least, can read without continuously moving their lips. Mrs Thatcher is a frequent visitor but then so is Mr Enoch Powell.

The reputation I had won as a backbencher enabled me to stand for, and win, the Chairmanship of the Bow Group in the spring of 1966. I beat Hugh Dykes. I made it my custom to entertain the Group's speakers to dinner at my club, the Carlton, before the meeting. All went well until I gave Jo Grimond dinner. The meal passed without incident, but a day or two later I received a summons to attend upon the Chairman of the club, Lord Grimston, who had sat for Westbury in the Commons. The appointment was for one o'clock (there was no mention of lunch) and I was regrettably but unavoidably late. Grimston had gone but his disapproval was made very plain. I asked my friends for their advice: Leon Brittan thought the whole affair absurd; but David Windlesham did not: 'You should never entertain at your club someone you could not put up for membership of it.' I expect he was right, although, somewhat ironically, a week to the day after I dined Grimond, Ted Heath gave lunch at the Carlton to Kosygin. I joined the Garrick.

The Bow Group, which has always been first generation public school and Oxbridge, used to be on the left of the party. Today it is more likely to be of the right, having taken its place in the ranks of the party's *arditi*, and its tone from the prevailing orthodoxy. In my time as Chairman, the favourite term of approbation was 'X has gravitas', which suggests that we were pretty insufferable. Mind you, gravitas is a condition to which I have for a long time secretly aspired. Patrick Jenkin, who was a very grave young man, once went so far as to accuse me of levitas. We ran into each other in the Westminster Underground station. Patrick was clearly enraged and it was not long before I discovered why. *Crossbow,* the Group's quarterly, had just been published and on its cover was a photograph of a pretty Young Conservative (who, it so happened, was the secretary of the editor of the *Sunday Times*), wearing nothing but a man's shirt, an outrage for which the magazine's editor, Mr Leon Brittan, was responsible. Patrick's parting shot, before the train doors closed mercifully upon him, was a request for 'plain brown envelopes in future', which helps to put the 'swinging sixties' into perspective.

The favourite topic of Bow Groupers was candidate selection, for we were all desperately on the make. We would bump into one another in the dingy offices of North and East London Conservative Associations, seated to the smell of cat on the hardest of chairs, waiting nervously for our summons to sing and dance. How we must have patronised those local worthies with our references to *Sybil* and *Coningsby* and by our careful disregard of their prejudices.

Not so today. Whereas it was once the duty of the Conservative MP to filter the views of the constituents, today he has become their megaphone, for the party has, in recent years, moved closer to a state of nature. The businessmen with flat, provincial accents who, a decade or more ago, at Brighton or Blackpool, pressed strongly for greater competition; small town surveyors and estate agents, the politically active middle class which began by taking over the constituency parties, have now taken over Parliament itself. The *petit embourgeoisement* of the Conservative Party and its reversion to a form of nineteenth century Liberalism have gone hand in hand.

5   Making Ends Meet

In October 1964 I went down at Rochester to Mrs Anne Kerr, the Labour candidate who today would be regarded as of the 'soft left' but twenty years ago was very much on the far left of the party, by a thousand votes. It was a bitterly fought election, a re-run almost of the multilateralist/unilateralist arguments which had riven the Labour Party in the early sixties. Mrs Kerr, handsome but *simpliste*, had been selected as candidate by one vote in a town with a 'patriotic' Labour vote, drawn largely from the dockyard. After the dust had settled I was that most wretched of creatures, the ex MP, cut off abruptly from the routs and rallies of Westminster, and, what was more, with no visible means of support. I was determined to get back into Parliament, but the question was how.

Given the size of Harold Wilson's majority (four; shortly to be reduced to two) another general election was bound to take place quickly. Should I stay on at Rochester or try for a safer seat elsewhere? As my divorce was pending, I had no choice but to stay put. That was easier said than done, for my independence was none too popular with the more conventional members of the local party, while my support for the abolition of retail price maintenance in what was largely a shopkeepers' seat, had not endeared me to the Rotarians of Rochester. And the local paper was hostile, not least because of my support for the Common Market. The Executive Committee of the local party met and recommended my re-adoption and I duly appeared before a Special General Meeting of the whole association.

The ride promised to be a rough one, and in anticipation ballot papers had been prepared. A crowd of two hundred forsook the telly for what promised to be a more exciting entertainment. I spoke, but it was not my tongue that saved me. An unknown in the audience rose to his feet at the start of the meeting and attacked me personally ('party representatives need to set a high moral tone . .'). As if by magic the atmosphere changed, friends rallied to me and no vote was taken. In his book *The Selectorate*, Peter Paterson wrote of this event: 'Thoroughly petit bourgeois and narrowly unrepresentative of the community at large, riled no doubt by some of Critchley's policies and attitudes, and possibly worried by the imponderable electoral effects of his divorce, which had just become public, the committee nevertheless recommended his readoption as the prospective candidate.' And at the larger meeting of two hundred I was lucky in my enemy. One result of the affair was that one part at least of the folklore of candidate selection joined the past: 'that the selectorate, particularly in Conservative Associations where women predominate, invariably take a thoroughly illiberal attitude over the private lives of politicians.'

And I had only Anne Kerr to beat, which I failed to do in the spring of 1966, going down by two thousand votes. I bade farewell to the Medway Towns, where I had spent nine years either as candidate or Member, and drove to London. I had my living to make.

After the defeat in '64 I had become a freelance journalist. In 1965 I turned down an invitation from Gavin Astor's *Times* to become the paper's defence correspondent, as it would have meant not fighting the '66 election: a year later the rule and the owner had changed, the post, incidentally, having gone to Charles Douglas-Home, the present editor of the paper. Instead I became the defence correspondent of the *Glasgow Herald*, the nursery for many of Fleet Street's better known scribblers. I never set foot in Glasgow but only in the paper's London office where, for several years, I handed in my copy to a nice old Scot called David White. The *Herald*, together with a modest fee from Rosenthal whose china I puffed in the columns of the smarter women's magazines, kept body and soul, and, having married Heather Goodrick in the summer of '65, we took the top floor of a house in Notting Hill Gate which was owned by Michael Heseltine.

At that time Michael Heseltine, having lost money in

property in the early sixties, was recouping his fortunes through the Haymarket Press which he owned. In '64 he had fought and failed to win the Labour seat of Coventry North but in the '66 election he had succeeded Sir Henry Studholme as the Tory MP for Tavistock. I had passed him on his way up, coming down. Although I had taken no part in his business activities, I was, I suppose, his closest friend; at least I was invited to be his best man at his wedding to Anne Williams. As is customary, we both made speeches, an occasion at which we were probably at our worst. Elspeth Howe, the wife of Geoffrey, was heard to observe from behind a curtain. 'What a couple of * * *'. She could have been right.

After my second defeat Michael asked me whether I would become editor of *Town*, the glossy men's magazine (this was before the age of soft porn) in which I had so ill-advisedly appeared some years earlier, the flagship of his clutch of publications. Unwisely, as it turned out, I agreed, stepping into the better paid shoes of the existing editor who was sacked to make room. *Town* had begun life four years previously as *Man about Town* (later *About Town*) and had glittered for a time; what I did not know then was the fact that it had never made a penny profit. It had had a series of editors, at the rate of one a year, which should have put me on my guard; but it was nevertheless an attractive offer and well timed, for my contract with Rosenthal was not renewed and the *Glasgow Herald* was not very profitable. I accepted.

In the spring of 1984 the magazines of the sixties was the theme of an exhibition held at the ICA. *Town*, its covers and some of its photo-journalism, was given pride of place. I have carefully kept my dozen issues which, upon re-inspection, shrink in size as the year progressed. I commissioned pieces from the young Jill Tweedie and an even younger Jeffrey Bernard and sent Cyril Ray to cover the opening of the Playboy Club. But whatever the quality of the writing, or, indeed, the layout, for *Town* was always a good looking product, the monthly contributors' budget was cut, and I was left making do with pieces commissioned and paid for, but not used, by my predecessors.

As the rate of descent quickened we did discuss whether or not our girls should be naked. By 'naked' I did not mean the kind of pictures, gynaecologically explicit, which are commonplace in today's men's magazines, but the sort of romanticised nudity which can be found in say the *Sunday Times* colour supplement. But there is, or was, a Swansea side to Michael, a valleys prudishness which reinforced his feelings of apprehension lest his political career be damaged by the charge of pornography. A copy of *Town* with a girl on the cover had been brandished at an election meeting in some Devon market town, much to the candidate's apparent embarrassment. To his credit or not, he did not permit me to make the magazine more sexually attractive to its audience of 'young executive males' (indeed, he was for ever complaining about what sex there was in the magazine): in consequence, the writing was plainly on the wall.

Several factors had combined to erode our friendship. The fact that I was beholden to him, and, out of the House, in no position to share, or even sustain, his own political

progress within it, and, to be fair, his own financial anxiety — which he did not share with me — about the magazine. The old intimacy had gone. The fact that we shared the same house, the Critchleys living on the top floor and the Heseltines in the rest, probably did not help. In the event I tried unsuccessfully to become the editor of the *Listener* (it went to Karl Miller), and Michael began a discreet campaign, always at second hand, to force me out. After eleven months as editor I was finally sacked and given a month's money and Brian Moynahan put in my place. But *Town* was wound up six weeks later.

It was the most humiliating period of my life. In just over two years I had lost my seat, my job, and my oldest friend. My wife and I were obliged to sell our flat back to Michael (at the price we had paid for it fifteen months previously) and move to a rented cottage in Shamley Green owned by the Bransons, parents of Richard. It was William Rees Mogg who came to the rescue. He wrote to say that he admired my efforts to make a success of *Town* and asked me to become a regular contributor to his paper, writing a twice weekly column of television criticism together with Michael Billington and a monthly political column. Years later I interviewed Michael at the Carlton Club for some paper or other. I asked him whether he had ever made a mistake. 'Yes,' he said, 'sacking you.'

Besides writing pieces for *The Times*, hidden away in the depths of the Surrey hills, I wrote begging letters to chairmen of Conservative Associations who were in search of a candidate. One by one, friends and enemies who had sat with me in the Commons were picked for safe seats but the postman stayed away from my door. Then in the summer of '68 I had a letter from Reigate asking if I would appear.

The Reigate selection process was one of the first of the very few 'open primaries' which the Tory Party has ever held. The short list was decided after an interview and from the last six (Howe, Chataway, Peter Thomas, Anthony Meyer, myself and David Walder), Howe and Chataway were picked to meet in the final, which was to be filmed by Thames Television's *This Week* and reported by me for the *Sunday Times*. The contest, which was an intriguing one, was to be decided by the votes of paid up members of the

Association, and the champions were evenly matched. Geoffrey Howe had been in the House for two years and on the front bench, losing his seat in '66: Chataway had been a junior Minister in the Macmillan Government. They were the most promising of the younger Tories, Howe right wing at least on economic matters, Chataway excessively 'moderate'. They were given twenty minutes each followed by questions, and their wives five. Six hundred people, most of them women, made up the audience.

Howe won, but only on points. He was thoughtful and his appeal to the party activists — 'people who care about our country and want to do something about it' — was well judged. Chataway was the more sophisticated but visibly nervous. The wives provided a telling contrast. Anna Chataway was perhaps a shade too 'West End' for the mid-Surrey middle class, but Elspeth Howe got it right. 'What politicians need is a certain sort of love,' she declaimed, and there was not a dry eye in the house.

After Reigate I had to wait six months until I received another letter, this time from the Rugby Conservatives, a seat which Labour had won in '64 and held two years later. While it was no better than Rochester would have been, it seemed to offer my only chance. After an interview, where I spotted the young Jeffrey Archer and his pretty wife, I was invited to contest the final and my wife and I drove from my uncle's house in Sussex in the teeth of a blizzard, arriving at the hall five minutes before proceedings were due to start. My speech went well but the questions were all about race. I had retained enough of my Liberalism not to equivocate, and I did not give to many the answers they sought. I lost, but then so did the Rugby Tories in 1970.

After so narrow an escape, I next received a letter from the Wimbledon Tories who were looking for a successor to the redoubtable moralist and low churchman, Sir Cyril Black. I was summoned to an interview by some party functionary who, looking hurriedly through my biographical details, spotted the word 'divorce'. 'That won't do for Wimbledon,' he said. A fortnight later it was reported that he had left home with the au pair girl. But Wimbledon, like Reigate, opened up the final to the press, an event which I attended for *The Times*.

This time it was a battle for hearts and minds between Michael Havers, who was the favourite from the start, Ian Gow and my friend David Walder. David was never at his best on his feet and his response to the question 'What are your views on drugs, crime and pornography?', which was 'I am against them', was deemed to show a degree of rectitude that clearly lacked relish. He was swiftly eliminated. Ian Gow, who was later, as PPS to Mrs Thatcher, to become her Great Chamberlain, delivered a fundamentalist speech of such a dizzy eloquence, out-Blacking, as it were, Sir Cyril himself, that the electors of Wimbledon were sorely tempted to break ranks. It was to their credit that they stayed put.

I had to wait another six months before I heard from Aldershot. Sir Eric Errington was retiring, would I allow my name to go forward? I learnt later that all former Tory MPs had been invited to do so. Aldershot I saw as my last chance, for by then most of the hundred Tory MPs who had lost their seats at the two previous elections, had been suited. I asked Philip Goodhart for his advice. It was to this effect: too many aspirants make the mistake of making a predictable political speech attacking Harold Wilson and sliding over the discrepancies in Tory policies, when what Selection Committees really want is local knowledge and concern. How wise he was.

At his bidding I rang the editor of the local paper and journeyed (for the first time) to Aldershot, where I spent a day with him. I was briefed, and a couple of days' work enabled me to speak to the Executive Committee of the local Tories with some authority about the constituency, its problems and peculiarities. It was good advice. I was marked top in three separate stages and beat Colin Turner, who had sat for Woolwich, in the final. I had been chosen for a safe seat. And I had not even served in the army, unlike several of my rivals, who claimed to have 'crawled over every inch of it'.

I had the impression that I would not have been Eric Errington's choice, but he was kind, permitting me to buy him a large lunch at the Garrick. In the '66 election, so I was told, Eric had addressed a meeting in Fleet. Age had taken its toll, and during that campaign he was escorted everywhere by two stalwart Young Conservatives whose task it was to help him to his feet at public meetings. An act of levitation took place after which Eric began his speech by saying, 'Mr Chairman, I have difficulty getting up, but once I have done so I'm as good as ever I was . . .' By all accounts, and I have heard several, his audience of colonels and their ladies collapsed with laughter.

But it was not until later that I learnt that there could have been a hiccup in my selection. Midway through the selection procedures, Central Office had asked the Association to drop everything and adopt John Davies, but had been politely refused. And a prominent Tory woman asked for the

inclusion of the young Winston Churchill, which was also refused. The same woman then asked the President of the Association, Sir Richard Gough Calthorpe, whether he knew I had been divorced. 'I do, and so what?' was his reply. I had my share of luck.

What then are the qualities needed for adoption as a Tory candidate? I am tempted to say persistence but there is a little more to it. It does not much matter whether you are to the left or right for the Tory Party is not yet an ideological party, and much prefers courtesy and conventionality. Despite the stridency which has crept into party pronouncement and personality, Selection Committees still pick on ability and amiability. And wives are important. A nice old colonel from Fleet once asked me if I knew why I had been chosen. Nervously, I said no. 'It was your wife,' he said. 'Damned fine woman. And the only one of them to stand up when we asked her a question.'

But it is fifteen years since I was subject to the necessary impertinence of candidate selection. I had few qualifications, save a quick tongue, a public school accent and a well mannered wife. I had never commanded men in battle, run a great company or made (as opposed to earned) money. I just wanted to get into Parliament. Apparently it was enough.

Perhaps the last word on candidate selection should go to Geoffrey Dickens, an eccentric Conservative MP who once, when a soldier, boxed eight rounds against Don Cockell. Boundary changes necessitated his seeking a new seat. He showed me the notes of the speech he had made in which he had persuaded the burghers of Littleborough and Saddleworth to pick him. The notes read: (a) twenty years of ceaseless fight against Socialism (b) flogging and hanging and (c) Mrs Thatcher.

6   *La Politique de Vacances*

Some MPs are sent to Europe. I was approached in December '72 by John Stradling Thomas, one of our Whips, and asked whether I would like to become a delegate to the Council of Europe and the Western European Union. He told me it meant lots of travel and a tax-free income. Tempted on both counts, I agreed to serve, and for seven years until the first Thatcher election victory, I struggled to and from Heathrow Airport, that *anus mundi*, in order to attend political meetings of small importance in congenial countries across the globe. It was all a terrible waste of time.

Mind you, it had its moments. The Council of Europe, formed in 1949 in the heady days of European unity, consisted of all the respectably democratic countries of Europe; its assembly of nominated politicians met three times a year in Strasbourg where it took a high moral tone while touring *les routes des vins*. It was a boring place preoccupied by things of marginal importance. The Western European Union met twice a year in Paris, a second assembly made up of the same place-men, the child of the revised Brussels Treaty of 1954 in which Britain, France, Germany, Italy and the Benelux pledged to come to each others' help in the event of war. The Council of Europe met in January, May and October; the Western European Union in December and June. Each assembly spawned many committees which, in their turn, trod the light fantastic, turning up in Athens or Atlanta in pursuit of some report, which would then be debated at a meeting of the assembly. It was, and still is, the political equivalent of Arthur Conan Doyle's Red-Headed League.

The Tories had, by the early seventies, come to regard membership of these twin bodies either as reward for services rendered (usually silent), or as a form of exile; out of sight, out of mind. I could not claim to belong to the first category. The expenses of travel were all borne by the tax-payer, and each delegate was given a per diem allowance which today is the equivalent in francs of £70. It was not enough to live like Riley but free meals and generous hosts left a margin which could be spent on little delicacies, brought home to neglected wives. In '72, the leader of the Conservative delegation of eighteen — there were a total of 36 British delegates, with the balance divided between the other two major parties — was Simon Wingfield Digby, a Dorset landowner of the old school. He was to be succeeded first by Sir John Rodgers, the MP for Sevenoaks, a nice old thing of a remarkable conviviality, and finally by Sir Frederic Bennett of Torquay.

If the composition of the Tory team had something of the flavour of *la deuxième cru,* it had not always been so. In the great days after the war, the leaders of the party went to Strasbourg. Churchill, Eden, Macmillan, Boothby: their yellowing photographs can still be found in the remoter corridors of the Palais de l'Europe, their faces flushed by *les vins d'Alsace* in the congenial company of de Gasperi, Paul Henri Spaak and Robert Schuman. They would have travelled by train from Paris, pulled by great, black Pacific locomotives, travelling swiftly through a darkening country-side, lulled by the gentle tinkling of glass upon glass. We flew from Heathrow in a charter 'plane, clutching free bottles of Ma Griffe, not all of which reached home, a cheerful body of schoolboys in pursuit of *la politique de vacances.*

The Labour Party, which was inclined to bring crates of beer to put in the back of the bus, shuffled its pack more frequently than we did, and thus tended to pick better people. Socialists came and went; Tories on the other hand, unless they made a nuisance of themselves by borrowing, and forgetting to pay back, could stay on the delegation for as long as they liked. Many grew old in the restaurants of Strasbourg.

I was attracted by the money, the travel and by the chance to study defence at the WEU, defence being my subject. I took Paris seriously and was elected Chairman of the assembly's Defence and Armaments Committee where I wrote, with the help of Stuart Whyte, the committee's clerk,

more reports on esoterica than any of my predecessors. It did me no good, but I enjoyed it. The Council of Europe, on the other hand, I treated lightly. I neglected the assembly, a body with a high moral content which rose to the spirit of the times by admitting Liechtenstein to the comity of nations, after which the prime movers were awarded funny medals by a funny Grand Duke. But I fell in love with Strasbourg.

It was Ernie Bevin who, on being told that the Strasbourgeois spoke French from nine to five and German at home, determined that the city should become the 'capital' of Europe, despite the worst climate in France, poor communications, true even of today, and wines of a high acidity, even when not drunk to excess. The old city has charm, encircled by water, its black and white buildings carefully restored after suffering the damage of three wars. It is dominated by its one-spired cathedral, on the top of which infrequent storks build their nests. The Tories were encouraged to stay at a newly-built hotel, comfortable, expensive and characterless. The hotel's restaurant, where I ate once a visit, was famous for its frogs' legs and *oeufs à la neige*; the hotel itself was, on occasion, in trouble with the police, as the telephoned request by Knights of the Shire for 'deux oreillers' had been known to result in the arrival not of two pillows but of two *filles de joie*. It was not for that reason that I decided to stay elsewhere.

I scoured the old city for a cheaper and prettier hotel, an act of desertion which caused much huffing and puffing. I found the Gutenberg, once the favourite hotel of the Wehrmacht, an early nineteenth century family-run establishment in a corner of the square opposite the cathedral. I made room number 8 my own, a chamber on the first floor in which there was a double bed with a crown at its head from which hung faded yellow drapes on which buzzed the Imperial bees. I kept a bottle of Riesling in the bidet. It was to there that I would return late at night to sleep fitfully, roused by the bells of the city, troubled by *matelot à la crème*, onion tart and knuckle of pork, the whole churning rebuke watered by the mouth-puckering *vins de pays*. Those were the days.

I did not live entirely for pleasure. The twin hazards of political life abroad are boredom and the remorseless hospitality. I can put up with a day in Brussels, even two if it means dining at Comme Chez Soi, but five nights of *vins d'honneur*, garrulous foreigners (of the very best sort) and one's colleagues, can not only be wearying but a monumental waste of time. But Brussels, despite its smell of expensive chocolate and small cigars, is not life-enhancing, although the national dish of *moules aux frites* has much to recommend it. Ten years ago I could put up with a week of parties in Strasbourg or Paris; today, I have learnt to husband my resources.

At the start I did attempt to take the Council of Europe

seriously. In those days it was housed in a prefabricated building opposite a suburban park inside which was a good restaurant and a poor zoo. In the corridor outside a café inside which the delegates would spend the greater part of their time, was a machine which, when its button was pressed, would play part of the last movement of Beethoven's Choral Symphony, long adopted by enthusiasts as Europe's national anthem. The sound of the hymn of joy can be guaranteed to bring back the taste of crusty ham sandwiches, bitter black coffee and the desultory gossip of friends and enemies.

I prepared my maiden speech carefully, although I have forgotten its theme. I began by reminding the assembly of the dictum of Henri V, the Holy Roman Emperor, that he spoke French to his wife, Italian to his mistress, and German to his horse. I shocked the interpreters, but my audience, which consisted of a scattering of octogenarian Belgian stationmasters, remained unmoved, having succumbed to the effects of a six-course lunch at the Crocodile.

La cuisine strasbourgeoise is as robust as it is tasty, although its wines are inclined to be liverish. The food is French and the size of the helpings German. The British in general, and the Tories in particular, would lunch nearly every day at Le Bourse aux Vins, an old-fashioned bistro next door to the Sofitel, presided over by a noisy Madame and her pretty daughter. It was invariably full of locals scoffing onion tart. I made friends with Michael St Helens, who, as Michael Hughes Young, the Deputy Chief Whip in the early sixties, had put a stop to my becoming a Parliamentary Private Secretary. He claimed not to be able to remember the episode. He was old, lonely and very deaf, but very good on the subject of the Liberation of Brussels by the Guards Armoured Division in 1944. 'I was shot in the arse by a jealous husband.' I would like to think that it was true. Eventually, Le Bourse was bought up by a jealous Sofitel, whose lunchtime trade languished in comparison, but the hotel was sensible enough not to disturb Madame.

I took advantage of my annual three weeks in Strasbourg to recharge batteries, after a time picking which invitation to accept, sitting in the open air in cafés, sipping Gewurtztraminer and gazing at the distant blue line of the Vosges, lunching sometimes alone, making sure that when evening came my companions were congenial. On Sundays we would be taken to some castle, the most popular of which was the Kaiserhof, built for Kaiser Bill when Alsace was still part of the Second Reich. We would take lunch and then be ferried to some safari park where before a large audience of natives, a serpent would be tossed at the feet of a secretary bird which would promptly stamp on its head and then swallow it to much Gallic applause. In October we would tour the wine-making villages, where, to the pumping of village bands, we would take our battered livers to task by sampling the vintage. Lunch in Colmar, tea in Baden Baden, and, best of all, dinner in some village hotel on locally caught fish; there were compensations for so much oratory, much of which was happily incomprehensible.

Besides the admission of Liechtenstein two other events stand out. The speech by Mintoff who happened to be the Chairman of the Council of Ministers. Unattractive, self-serving and belligerent, he was given the bird, not a single socialist attempting to come to his assistance; and the opening by Giscard of the Palais de l'Europe in '76 built to replace our prefabrication. As ceremonies go it was very grand, although not as grand as the opening of the Odeon, Swiss Cottage by Merle Oberon and Alexander Korda in the summer of 1939. The Palais does resemble an Odeon with each of its many floors painted a different colour, a hemicycle fit for Demosthenes, as many committee rooms as there were delegates and, on my most recent visit in the spring of 1984, a barber's with the prettiest girl I can remember. One could sleep in the Palais as well as anywhere in Strasbourg.

I enjoyed attending the WEU in Paris rather more. Visits in either December or June meant returning to Paris at times of extremes of temperature. I have been hotter and colder in Paris than in any other city. The Western European Union has its headquarters in the ugliest building in the city on the Avenue Wilson (Woodrow not Harold) in the 8th arrondissement. I was, after all, revisiting, and at someone else's expense, the most beautiful city in the world, where, twenty years before, I had spent time as a student. However hard the seats in the Avenue Wilson, or brutal the tapestries, or dull the speeches (and the dullest, by far, was the one given all too frequently by Joe Luns, the Secretary General of Nato, who invariably switched from English to French to German without his audience being any the wiser) outside was Paris. I would introduce my report, sum up at the end of the debate, and then vanish into the city like some public school Proust.

Once when I was speaking from the rostrum a clerk passed me a note which read, 'Lunch with me, Gladwyn.' I was happy to do so. We drove, via the British Embassy where Lord Gladwyn had served with such distinction some years previously, to his club in the Marais, so smart, rumour had it, that only relations of Giscard were members. While we drank an aperitif, we were approached by a nervous waiter who inquired whether a table had been booked. Gladwyn looked him in the eye and said, 'Je suis l'ancien ambassadeur anglais en France . .' The waiter withdrew. Upon our second aperitif I noticed a more senior figure plucking up courage to speak to my host. 'Une table, c'est impossible. You have not paid your subscription since . .' Gladwyn raised himself to his full height and replied, 'Je suis l'ancien ambassadeur de la Reine Britannique en France.' The steward collapsed and we were shown promptly to a table. The lunch, which was as good as Gladwyn's sang froid had been admirable, must have been very expensive indeed.

During the early seventies I stayed at several different hotels, more often than not revisiting my old haunts in the Quartier Latin, taking a room in the Hôtel des Saints Pères. Nothing seemed to have changed. There were still the drab, brown-painted cafés with their zinc bars, the green crosses of chemist shops and the incivility of the Parisians, rivalled only in curmudgeony by the inhabitants of New York. One thing had changed; the klaxons, against a background of which Gene Kelly had danced, and fallen silent, victims of the rigours of the Fifth Republic.

Later I stayed at small hotels in the 8th and 16th, closer to the Trocadero and the Assembly. If a debate were even duller than I expected, I would take the Métro and recapture the journeys of my youth when I had a room near the Gare de L'Est and the girl with whom I was in love a room at La Muette. I am certain that neither my children nor hers would permit sixteen *stations de Métro* to come between them and their heart's desire.

While returning home I ran into Frank Laws Johnson, who had been my bank manager in Paris in the fifties, and whose daughter had been a close friend. From then on I was welcome to stay with the Laws Johnsons at Neuilly. Frank is a lover of wine and, as is the case with wine buffs, eager to share his treasures. Twice a year, on the occasion of my visits, he would have a dinner party for his French and expatriate English friends. My diary, which I would like to think resembles Alan Clark's in being a record of 'lechery, malice and self pity' seems to contain only a record of wines drunk. For example, at one party they were as follows: Champagne Mercier '61, Meursault '44, Calon Ségur '24, a magnum of Cheval Blanc '47 (described by Hugh Johnson as 'the finest claret ever bottled') and a Montrose '22. I was drinking far above my station.

Thus for seven years I ate, drank, slept and scribbled in two French cities. We urged the rationalisation of European arms procurement ten years before the idea became a cliché. With the help of a retired German General we redrew Nato's line of battle on the Central Front and, in good time for the 'twin track decision' taken by the Nato Council in '79, drew attention to the Soviet build-up of intermediate range missiles, the SS20s. The documents, presented, debated and passed, usually against the opposition of the French, went unnoticed. My reward was a lunch, given twice a year, at one of the best restaurants in Paris.

Recently, the WEU has caught the public eye, and there is talk of the organisation being given a new role in the search for a European defence 'identity', the purpose of which would be to reassure American opinion which tends to believe that rich Europeans are being defended from poor Russians by Americans; and, at the same time, to reassure European public opinion by demonstrating that collective security is not the sole responsibility of President Reagan. That WEU has lived quietly in London and Paris for thirty years, doing harm to no-one, cannot be denied. It is also true that from time to time WEU has been rediscovered by lascivious Frenchmen who flirt outrageously à la Jobert with the old body, seeing in it the means whereby a French or even an exclusively Franco-German view of European defence could be created. More recently, it has been awakened with a kiss from M Claude Cheysson, the French Foreign Minister. I cannot help wondering ruefully whether he might not, after all, make a decent woman of the old body and lead her to the altar. But I have my doubts; the French are fickle.

I suppose that service in Europe cured me of any wish to stand for the European Parliament. Seven years of fog-bound airports, incomprehending constituents and peripheral concerns have cured my itchy feet. The action, such as it is, takes place at home. I gained in knowledge, and in confidence, and the money saved by a regime of lunchtime omelettes (in the absence of an invitation to lunch at somebody else's expense) helped with the school fees. But I stayed abroad too long. While I scoured the kiosks for the *Herald Tribune*, Margaret Thatcher defeated Ted Heath in the Peasants' Revolt of '75, the Conservative Party took on a Cromwellian tinge, and my contemporaries won preferment. I would have done better to stay put and congratulate Shadow Ministers on the quality of their speeches. It was foolish but it was fun.

7   A Foot in a Thousand Doors

Candidates love elections; MPs do not.

If an MP tells you he enjoys elections, do not believe him, for he is not telling the truth. Candidates may look forward to elections: they have, after all, waited anxiously since their adoption, spoken to small meetings of party activists and bombarded the local press with handouts purporting to show knowledge, competence and concern. A general election may transform their lives, taking them out of dead-end jobs to a seat high up at the very back of the Government back benches. The magic initials may be theirs.

If in life perspective is all, then the MP must take a very different view. Neurotic enough at the best of times, he bids a long farewell to the Palace of Westminster inside the walls of which he has spent long hours at the behest of the party Whips, and to which he was sent, five years ago, in order to escape the real world. A Last Supper with colleagues at which all too familiar faces become almost beguiling, and the cut off the joint with two veg (either over or under-cooked) takes to itself something of the magic of Elizabeth David. An afternoon spent tidying up his office, a tiny room, tucked away under the roof, where everything can be regulated save the temperature, and a last look at the Chamber, the cock pit of the nation where his occasional ten minute contribution has been subjected to the slings of his peers and the arrows of Frank Johnson and Michael White.

Elections are hell. Three weeks of fatigue, boredom and anxiety in which his days are spent 'on the knocker' (Dame Patricia Hornsby-Smith once startled New York by confessing on prime time television to having spent her election days 'knocking up'), or, if young, running from house to house in order to impress the media, and his nights in draughty village halls talking up the Prime Minister. Unlike by-elections, where the candidates are illuminated by the attention of the press and television, at a general election the candidate is generally ignored; even the local papers are more interested in Aldershot's Saturday night fever than they are in reporting the election.

I have fought eight general elections, winning six of them. This is less a tribute to me than a comment upon the class nature of British politics. Rochester and Chatham was a working class seat with a small but growing middle class; in the late fifties and early sixties, the exodus into Waits houses had not yet reached its flood, and wages, in Chatham at least, were depressed by the dockyard. In Aldershot, however, the demography was different. The seat is called Aldershot, but in 1970 it extended westwards into the villages of north-east Hampshire, to Odiham and Hartley Wintney where the cottages were lived in by the rich and retired, and to the small town of Fleet in which army officers and their wives had taken refuge, in many cases buying property long before retirement. Aldershot itself is primarily a working class town, the home of non-commissioned officers, many of whom have set themselves up in small businesses. But, working class or not, the vote has a strongly patriotic flavour, as one would expect, and, when taken with Farnborough, which is more middle class than Aldershot, the outcome was a safe Tory seat; indeed 'Aldershot', however defined, has never returned anyone save for a Conservative since the seat came into being in the 1880s. As 'Mr' Critchley, I succeeded Sir Eric Errington, who had, in his turn, taken over from Lord Chandos.

An election in a marginal seat such as Rochester was, inevitably, more exciting. It was not just the uncertainty of the result. Marginal seats received the full attention of Conservative Central Office which despatched into Kent a series of great men whose oratory was designed to bolster my chances. In Aldershot, we were totally ignored.

A curious thing about fighting an election in a safe seat like Aldershot is the sense of isolation from events. News filters into the town as if into a city besieged. There are no great men, or women, bringing news of the wider world. And, by the same token, you are bound within the limits of the constituency, driving ceaselessly from place to place, watching for the colour of the window bills, plunged into gloom by the sight of an orange or red. The evenings are spent preaching to the converted, or to their Labradors, which, on issues such as Rhodesia, were better behaved than their owners, or, and this happens at every election, the joint meeting with your opponents, with a Bishop in the chair.

A BACK BENCHER REPORTED IN THE PRESS

The National Union of Teachers play host to a bad-tempered meeting. The rare night without a meeting is spent canvassing, when, in answer to your insistent knocking, there is a slow drawing back of bolts, and the appearance of one hostile eye.

And yet, tiring though they are, elections have their moments. It is pleasant to leave Aldershot for the villages and to knock on cottage doors. In 1970, as in 1983, the election was held in the summer, and the rhododendrons were in bloom (all those soldiers and all that sand) and every porch framed in clematis. The occupants were polite, if wary, the more elderly having endured visits from importunate candidates at five yearly intervals for as long as they could remember. Every other cottage had been gentrified, its front door painted puce and the gate guarded

YOU MUST BE FROM MR CRITCHLEYS CONSTITUENCY...

by a Triumph Dolomite. For an hour at a time, the candidate is accompanied by a local supporter who knows the lie of land, one of whom will lunch with him at the local pub. In June 1983, I was invited to enter a long hut, the property of Mr Miles Hudson, the President of the local party, which was packed to the eaves with battery hens. Their heads poking through the bars they faced each other in their hundreds across an aisle, for all the world as if they were Members of Parliament. The air was filled with dust, the chamber reverberated to the noise of protest, petulance and pique: all that was needed was Mr Speaker with wattle and spurs. I shut the door swiftly upon such horrid symbolism.

I am a sensitive soul, for a politician that is, but in politics, it is necessary to grow a second skin. The politician tends to be either flattered or abused. At elections, I dread the first Monday of the three-week-long campaign, when the ancient Land Rover, lent for the duration by some friendly farmer, the flanks of which have been covered by misleadingly youthful pictures of the candidate, stands ready in the car park of the Conservative Club, with the party agent at the wheel. I stand beribboned like a bullock, microphone in one hand and leaflets in the other, waving sheepishly in the direction of bewildered housewives, making an ass of myself. But by Tuesday I no longer care, greeting smiles and scowls alike with a cheerful insouciance.

The candidate's time is carefully divided between the wards of the constituency. At the 1979 election I was given a minder whose task it was to collect me in the morning and return me late at night, dizzy with fatigue. His real purpose was to keep me out of mischief; if the candidate is propped up in the back of the Land Rover, or admiring an elector's dog, he or she cannot do anything that will get his or her name in the papers. Then my minder was a recently retired sapper general, but in '83, owing to the loss of Fleet at the hands of the Boundary Commission, his task was carried out by three stalwarts, none of whom had attained field rank.

In Aldershot, last time, I tramped the mean streets down by the station in the company of a friendly magistrate who, recognising from the electoral roll the names of those he had sent down, crouched in adjacent doorways while I rang their bells. Summoned, they grasped my hand, looked me straight in the eye and told me they were lifelong Tories. He marked them down as 'doubtful'. In one street I was told to be certain to call upon a particular woman. 'She has a mouth on her like the *Aldershot News*.' I did so, and she had; but what an epitaph.

With a foot in a thousand doors I keep an eye open for antiques. In an old people's home in Hawley I admired a Captain's Chest, handsomely bound in brass. 'Had a bloke in here the other day who offered me twenty quid for it.' It was worth two hundred. In the great houses of Eversley I won for myself a reputation for shiftiness, for my eyes would wander from beribboned matrons to their Baxters, while in Hartley Wintney, where every other shop sells antiques, the cottage which became the committee room contained a collection of more than fifty Staffordshire portrait figures including one of the murderer William Palmer. And in Farnborough, where the tree-lined streets are named after the forgotten courtiers of the Second Empire, I ran across a collection of 1887 Jubilee plates. I am tempted to become the Raffles of Mrs Thatcher's Conservative Party.

Is all the campaigning, the being-nice-to-people for so long, worth while? It is an exhausting business combining as it does unaccustomed physical exertion with the psychological strain of leadership, of projecting oneself from either platform or pavement. It is hard work being nice to people. I marvel at the stamina of the great: the sight of Michael Foot in the face of defeat and a few weeks off the age of seventy, humping his own suitcase to his front door; and Mrs Thatcher inexhaustibly feeding upon her zealotry. Success in politics is unobtainable without the possession of an athlete's stamina and the ability to drive oneself forward for yet another mile. General elections are clearly becoming more 'presidential', but for the foot soldiers of politics, what does it all achieve?

The task of the party candidate is to carry the party's banner. The language of elections is the language of war: campaigns are fought; elections won or lost. The role of the candidate is to put himself at the head of his troops, that small band of the party faithful, many of whom are friends

74

of long standing, who are untypical enough not only to care deeply about the future of their country, but to do something about it. At elections there is no place for qualification, no place for reasonable doubt; politicians regain that territory where the majority of us is most happy, the land of black and white. For three weeks out of every 260, it is a matter of my party right or wrong.

I do not think my activity, however frenetic, made any difference to my vote. In '83, I took fifty-five per cent. It was clearly impossible to meet, let alone impress, a significant proportion of an electorate which numbered nearly 80,000. I spoke at nine meetings, including two at which all three candidates performed, at which some 200 attended. About 400 came to the other seven, making a total audience of 800 out of 80,000 electors. Several thousand may have caught sight of my progress across Hampshire. So what? I was relying in a very small part upon my reputation locally: but ninety-five per cent on the national standing of the Conservative Party. For the first time in Aldershot, the Labour candidate lost his deposit, and I was chased into first place by an energetic young Liberal wielding a municipal drainpipe. By their votes, thirty-one thousand people had returned to Parliament someone who had been chosen thirteen years ago by 250, and reconfirmed (not reselected in the Labour Party sense) by say a hundred. Parliamentary democracy is certainly indirect.

What I was really doing over the election campaign was conducting a love affair with my own constituency party. At Westminster, you tend to lose touch. But you cannot expect others to work hard for you, and the party, if you do not, and the three to four weeks of campaigning gives an opportunity to rekindle old friendships and make new ones. Most of my active supporters are to the 'right' of me, especially on issues such as capital punishment, but the Tory coalition closed ranks, turning its guns upon our opponents. I might have been out at all hours and in all weathers, but I was accumulating credit in the bank.

Once the Member is returned to Westminster, it is surprising how undemanding local Conservatives can be. My supporters know that they have sent me to Westminster as the MP for Aldershot, and not the other way around;

although political enemies and opponents, especially the Liberals, sometimes try to make trouble on the grounds that 'he is never here', meaning in the constituency. The Liberals have adopted 'community politics' as a means of winning seats in Parliament, building occasionally upon their local government successes. But their candidate has to be very good; and the sitting Member, pretty bad. It is ironic that the very people who complain most about your alleged non-attendance, are those who are most eager to be rid of you.

The tendency to believe that the MP should be the 'Member for Westminster' in Aldershot has made little progress with Conservatives. MPs are not Mayors, County Councillors, District Councillors, Chief Executives, or even Traffic Wardens: their task is to represent their constituents of all persuasions and of none, and that can best be done at Westminster. The MP must be available. He will be expected to respond to invitations to lunch, to dine and to speak, and to pay visits to local institutions, such as hospitals, police and fire stations. He should, if he is wise, take the trouble to keep the local press informed of his activities. And today most, if not all, MPs hold 'surgeries' at weekly or fortnightly intervals.

At surgeries the MP makes himself available for inquiry and rebuke. In Tory seats, where the middle class predominates, attendance upon the Member can be slight; in working class seats, however, where most people cannot afford solicitors, and some cannot express themselves adequately on paper, the 'surgery' plays a greater part. In Aldershot, the majority of my customers come either in search of a council house (which I cannot give) or to bring a complaint of one kind or another against their neighbours, usually to do with planning permission (over which I have no jurisdiction). Where I can help is over social security payments, by speeding up the response of an over-worked local office of the DHSS, or by tackling the gas, electricity and water boards. Soldiers' wives sometimes come to see me to seek help in extracting their husbands from the Army. I do nothing until I see the soldier himself. After every election, the first surgery held does tend to attract the dotty who return at five yearly intervals for a chat. It is a small price to pay. A Miss O'Reilly was once ushered in at the end of a long and particularly arduous morning's work. I was drained of healing power. She began by saying that what she was about to tell me I would find hard to believe, which is always a bad sign. A cheerful woman of an uncertain age, she told me that she was the illegitimate daughter of the Duke of Windsor and would I intervene at the Palace on her behalf. But not all encounters are as hilarious, or as sad.

But the MP's relations with the local party are every bit as important. This will mean that Fridays (when the House is sitting) and weekends (all the year, save for August during which politics takes a holiday) can be taken up with wine and cheese parties, Fetes and Fayres, the annual general meetings of ward associations, and a plethora of Christmas parties. These can be tiresome, but are, more often, entertaining. I seem to have spent the best part of my life drawing the raffle.

The Conservative Party remains the non-political political party, despite all that has happened to it since Mrs Thatcher became its leader. MPs, leader writers and political commentators naturally take a vivid interest in politics, and, more particularly, in rival ideologies. Socialists do have 'socialism', an unreliable touchstone, I would have thought, but a touchstone of sorts: we do not. If the bulk of Tory activists are 'Thatcherite', it is not so in a political sense; they are simply loyal to the party's leader. When Mrs Thatcher became leader, the rank and file just switched loyalty from Ted Heath to his successor. I am sure my own party knows that I am a 'wet' but no one has ever attempted to argue me out of it. Politics is still left to the member.

The term 'wet' was coined by Mrs Thatcher in the early months of her first government as a description of those members of her cabinet who did not take to her economics. It is highly contemptuous, and, I suppose, rather offensive, but with a typically English insouciance it has been adopted, rather like the term 'desert rats' and 'old contemptibles' as a badge of honour. The word 'drys' is a less effective description; I prefer 'the arditi', the ardent ones, the ex-servicemen of post 1918 Italy, the precursors of fascism, who toured the country telling the Italians to pull up their socks.

Tory Party workers are by no means the behatted harridans so beloved of the cartoonist, ready with rope and rod. Some of my best friends are Tories. Thank God it is still more important in the Tory Party to turn up on time, be polite and assiduous than it is to hold to a set of political opinions, fashionable or no. No one in Aldershot has ever heard of intellectuals like Sir Alfred Sherman.

A general election campaign reaches its climax in the count. The candidates and their wives circle the floor, watching for the first signs of how the voting has gone; friends come up with transistors, bearing the results of other contests, the pattern of only one of which will be enough to tell you all you want to know. The row of bundled hundreds of ballots lengthens along the top table, each 'snake' a different colour. Thirty minutes or so before the final announcement, the result is known, and the counters, a proportion of whom will have worked for you, will be celebrating or commiserating as the case may be. Victory banishes all fatigue; defeat numbs the senses; whatever the end of it all, almost the best part of the whole 'beastly business' is the return home, a stiff drink and the telly, to sit and watch the fate of friends and enemies. It is the end of an ordeal by exposure.

8   Westminster Blues

I suppose an MP, if he so wished, could live indefinitely at the Palace of Westminster. One thousand rooms, a warren of obscure passages and hidden staircases of the sort used in Frascati by Cardinals to visit their lovers; even after twenty years I can stumble across strange lavatories and curious bars where aged peers talk to members of the lobby. The Palace is kept uncomfortably warm; somewhere in the bowels is a boiler, taken from a battleship, and, while the House is sitting at least, the alcohol flows freely. In recent years MPs have been given offices — the more senior have a room to themselves, with a sofa and an armchair. We are discouraged from plugging in percolators. Nevertheless, given a camp bed, the use of a telephone at the tax-payers' expense, light and heat and unlimited supplies of stationery, it is little wonder that on arrival, some of us, at least, are rarely seen or heard of again. And we have the best library in London where nice old things drop off while reading the *Spectator* only to wake to the sight of girls up ladders. There is a chained copy of *Private Eye* and a tendency among some of the stricter library girls not to permit novels to be supplied to Members. But even that proscription can be avoided. If it were not for the continual arrival of the post, life would be complete.

But there is the problem of where to eat, and, more particularly, with whom. At about half past twelve of a weekday morning, MPs cluster under the canopy in Old Palace Yard, waiting for the stream of taxicabs which will take them to yet another free lunch. Voices, either proletarian or proud, command conveyance to the Savoy or the Ritz, and the tribunes of the people quit the Palace of Westminster to toy with *filets de sole dieppoise* while listening with half an ear to the supplications of their hosts. For those of us who have received no invitation — and what is life but one humiliation after another? — we have no choice but to gather sadly in the Members' Dining Room, that Salon des Réfusés, in search of a crust and an unfamiliar face.

No politician is at his best on his feet. At Eatanswill and Westminster we are judged not by our words, or even by our deeds, but by our appetites. The officers of the Tory Party's Defence Committee lunch in the private rooms of smart restaurants with jolly generals, whose companies have something lethal to sell. The cable television lobby bash our ears over the creme caramel, Alasdair Milne tops up our glasses, while the television companies, at home in the Connaught, share with us their anxieties about the levy.

Foreign gentlemen at home in the Embassies ply us with sticky drinks. It is little wonder that the newly elected MP, who arrives at Westminster, trim from the rigours of electioneering, spreads remorselessly until, five years later, he sheds the effects of hospitality on the staircases of his electors.

There are one or two restaurants 'on the bell', that is, close enough to the Palace of Westminster to permit re-entry within seven minutes in order to vote in a division. Locketts is the best known. It is the haunt of the better sort of publicist and is famous for its 'lamb in the style of Shrewsbury', which, good though it undoubtedly is, has nothing in common with the mutton I ate for three and a half years at Shrewsbury School under the beady eye of Lord Wolfenden.

Eating at Westminster cannot be described as a gastronomic experience. Mr Clement Freud is not a regular attender. In recent years, the Chairman of the Kitchen Committee, the MP for Cheltenham, who is, in private life, an hotelier, has persuaded the Commons kitchen, not without difficulty for they are as touchy as Fleet Street printers, to provide a salad table of mixed hors d'oeuvres. The idea is a good one, although the table has suffered from the English disease of malt vinegar, so that every item tastes very much the same, which probably accounts for the diminution of the number of dishes, and the same might be said for the clientèle. But there is also a set lunch at a relatively modest price.

We are left, as it were, to tickle our own fancies. The success of lunch or dinner depends not upon the menu but upon one's neighbour, who can, if one is unlucky, have but one topic of conversation — the nature and extent of his ward boundaries. Members can be spied entering the dining room at a trot, subjecting the company, and in particular, the places left unoccupied, to an eagle-like *coup d'œil*; and then, having decided that the prospect is too dreadful to contemplate, disappearing by another door so as to reattempt the exercise in fifteen minutes' time. It is in this way that we work up an appetite.

It is now well known that we practise a kind of gastronomic apartheid, with the People's Party sitting at one end in shirtsleeves, eating gammon with pineapple chunks, while the Tories, whose jackets remain on however hot the weather, sit elsewhere, eating bloody beef and eggs in aspic. But I have never seen a bread roll thrown in anger. There is a Chief Whips' table, where I was once invited to dine. The clerks sit alone, lonely Wykehamists, talking of Michelangelo, as do the members of the Alliance. What is perhaps extraordinary is that this natural separation has not yet been applied to the divisions within the parties. Liberals still break bread with Dr David Owen, and Tory 'wets' still cringe when asked by new, and unrecognised, colleagues to pass the cruet. Both ends of the Labour movement can still be seen cheerfully dining together. And we are sometimes joined by junior Ministers who tell us about their red boxes and black Princesses and who tend to go on a bit about lights at the end of tunnels.

Humphry Berkeley used to dine with Barbara Castle on a mid-way table, drinking champagne out of pewter mugs and scandalising the old things of both parties. But such divertisements were rare.

The food can best be described as 'wholesome', still relatively cheap as it is subsidised by the taxpayer but the wine list is short with the most expensive item around six pounds. In the early sixties, the cellar was famously good, its contents accumulated over the years by a Wine Committee on which sat some of the grandest of the Tory Knights. But after the '64 election Robert Maxwell, then the Labour MP for Buckingham, was given the task of Chairman of the Kitchen Committee, and, in an attempt to balance the books, sold off the stock, substituting Grant's of St James. With every sip the older hands remember Bob Maxwell.

The only hazard is that the Prime Minister herself may join your table. Her appearance in the Members' Dining Room used to be signalled by the sight of Mr Ian Gow, the Abbé Mugnier of our great party, who, for many years as Mrs Thatcher's Parliamentary Private Secretary, did the rounds of the House of Commons for purposes of confession, absolution, extreme unction and entertainment. He has gone on to his reward, his place taken by St Michael Allison, whose task it now is to determine whether or not her neighbours are currently in a state of grace. The experience once befell me. A reverent hush fell upon the table and we sat silently to attention. 'Julian,' said Margaret, doing her

COMMONS SHOP *!#!

WHY
HAZARD
A LUNCH
WITH THE
P.M.?
INFLATABLE
COLLEAGUES
FOR THAT
EMPTY
CHAIR

FOLDS
FLAT
IN
SECONDS

Penelope Keith bit, 'what are your views on the money supply?' Lunches with Prime Ministers are rather like the annual Party Conferences: they tend to bring out the worst in your friends. The divisions within the Conservative Party are making life difficult for Michael Allison; one evening last December, the Prime Minister hovered at the door as the only tables with places vacant were occupied by Mr Edward Heath, Mr Francis Pym and Sir Ian Gilmour respectively.

But mealtimes can be fun. They are bazaars in which the latest political jokes can be exchanged. For example; 'What were Denis Thatcher's last words? There were none, his wife was with him till the end.' And 'I am screwing up my courage to tell Margaret that Jimmy Young isn't Jewish.' Sometimes we even talk sense. I once asked an aged Knight of the Shires, who was somewhat silent, whether, after a lifetime spent at Westminster, he would make any changes to the fabric of the Palace. Only one, he said. He would place photographs of women MPs in their underwear alongside the escalator which carries MPs up from their underground car park.

Twice a day we chart the rise and fall of the great ones, stand in silence in memory of Mr Patrick Jenkin, and say how well Mrs Edwina Currie performed in 'The Jewel and the Crown'. We mix malice with envy, and over carafes of Nigerian Burgundy, revenge ourselves for a lifetime spent at the beck of others.

The Members' Dining Room at the Commons is dedicated not to Freud but to Freud; it is the couch upon which we rid ourselves of our obsessions, purge our disappointments, sprinkle *schadenfreude* on our *sachertorte*, and escape our loved ones. At nine o'clock we sign our bills and depart, some for the Smoking Room, others to watch football on the telly, some even, those who have not yet seen everything, to the Chamber to listen to the wind-up.

Only the newly elected are regular attenders at Prime Minister's questions, which are held twice weekly on Tuesday and Thursday afternoons. Mrs Thatcher has views, many of which are unpalatable, and, in consequence, she is obliged to shout. Messrs Kinnock and Owen have also been known to raise their voices. The result is a cauldron of noise from which it is impossible to recognise good sense. The principal contenders are reinforced either by the gratuitously offensive from the Opposition benches below the gangway or by the obsequiously ambitious from the Government back benches. The effect is to provide entertainment for tourists (and distinguished foreigners who are expected to be favourably impressed), and copy for tomorrow's newspapers. The wise take their letters into the tea room in the confident expectation that lurking among the circulars will be one or more invitations to perform.

These can be divided into two: those performances for which payment will be made; and those for which it will not.

The first are invitations to sing and dance on behalf of the media, the second, to do so on behalf of friends. There is a third category, the invitation to perform within one's own constituency. I have been attending Mayoral banquets, Rotary lunches and Conservative Annual Dinners for as long as I can remember. Looking back they seem to have consisted of bowls of reconstituted tomato soup (the grains still clinging to the rim of the bowl), turkey (a bird that is as good as its stuffing) and a tinned peach perched on the top of a scoop of non dairy fat ice cream. And the rhetoric has been as memorable as the Spanish sauterne. I was asked to speak at a lunch given by the Rotary Club of Cranleigh. I spoke about the Common Market. Lunch consisted of roast beef which was overdone, Yorkshire pudding and mint sauce, and I swear I was the only one who noticed.

What can be as bad as the dinner is the dance. I once looked on dancing as a means to an end but time has put an end to that vanity. I now shuffle doggedly around the floor, enveloped in Chanel, to cheap music played far too loudly by a dozen yobs. As the dancers at Tory, and Mayoral, balls are without exception in what is known in Hartley Wintney as 'the prime of life', it is strange that we should be subjected to music of that kind. All I want is a bloke at the piano who plays nothing save Cole Porter, and a black girl singing. But I am told by the party's agents, who are responsible for these horrors, that nowadays only cheap music is cheap.

It is impossible to stay put in the Commons indefinitely. In order to sweeten our party workers upon whose benevolence our careers, such as they are, depend, we are obliged to accept the invitations of friends to perform in their backyards so as they, in their turn, will sing in ours. At any day, in any month of the year save August, when MPs are soaking up a foreign sun, MPs are searching desperately in the dark for the location of some dingy village hall in boring places like Bedfordshire, reshuffling their notes before singing for their supper.

I admit that I am not every Tory's cup of tea. I have yet to speak to the Women of Finchley, although I stand ready to give them a piece of my mind. The Conservatives of Blaby have sent no invitation winging my way, while the blue-haired widows of Suffolk Coastal have yet to ask me to lead them in prayer. But I have been to Amersham to speak on behalf of Sir Ian Gilmour.

We met for supper in a black-beamed hall belonging to the local party. On one whitewashed wall hung two pictures, one of Sir Ian looking remarkably cheerful, and one of Mrs Thatcher looking even more resolute than usual. I commented upon the novelty of this, but was assured by the party's agent that as much space as possible had been left between the two. The food was rather good, for the local Tories had had the good sense to abandon caterers with their plastic bags of *coq au vin*, and do the cooking themselves. Cheered by a casserole of *chicken à la norwegienne*, I spoke on sex and violence on the telly, being in favour of one and against the other. I make no great claim as to content but it can be more fun to talk about the telly, about which everyone has views, rather than bang on, as far too many of my colleagues do, about 'the resolute approach' or the 'future of the Common Agricultural Policy'. And the educated classes — and this was, after all, Gilmour territory — do feel threatened by Mr Clive James.

Performing before lunch and supper clubs is like boxing at the small halls, topping the bill at the West Ham Baths, drawing on a lifetime's experience to con the local Black Hope out of the decision. The constituency equivalent of the Empress Hall is to be invited to 'address' the Association Annual Dinner, where, poisoned by municipal caterers, the great men and women of the Conservative Party bring a message of hope to what can be, all too often, a dwindling band of supporters. We backbenchers are judged by the company we keep, or, to put it another way, by the distinction of the Guest of the Evening. It is an annual examination which not everyone is permitted to pass.

I am beginning to run out of people I can decently ask. Those members of Mrs Thatcher's Cabinet whom I found congenial have long been breaking stones on the back benches, while those who qualify as 'one of us' may be in no hurry to catch the 6.12 from Waterloo to Aldershot. But, in the past, we have done rather well. Cheered by the presentation of a bottle of La Tour '70 to mark his election victory of that year, Ted Heath spoke for forty minutes, and stayed as long chatting to Tories in the bar. Michael Heseltine came unprotected by car en route to his great house in Northamptonshire. He was subdued, as well he might, having returned from the Falklands the day before. He told the Aldershot Tories that when we were boys at the same prep school I had taken advantage of my age in order to sell him, at a grossly inflated price, a wooden model of a ship; an untypical failure on his part which no doubt set him on the road to his first million.

Members of Parliament do not just take in one another's washing. I go frequently to speak at Oxford or Cambridge. Last summer I dined at Sandhurst among scarlet-coated officers and much silver, the members of a staff college course. I told them that if I were ever to be made Secretary of State for Defence, which is unlikely, I would be remembered as a great reformer. I would hang a portrait of Leslie Hore-Belisha, who as Minister obliged the cavalry to take tanks in 1937, in my room at the Ministry of Defence, in the same way as Michael Heseltine took Orpen's portrait of Lloyd George with him when he left the Department of Environment for Defence. I would put a stop to army bands playing inside tents, strip the napkins off the bottles of wine, and put a stop to women soldiers marching. After thirty minutes of exhortation, and, having urged them à la Grimond to march towards the sound of gunfire, I was shown to my motor car by a senior officer. I asked who else they had invited to address them. 'Peter Tatchell and Ken Livingstone,' was the reply. 'We work on the basis of "know thine enemy".'

I enjoy debating against the Campaign for Nuclear Disarmament, especially against the Turbulent Priest, and visiting our great public schools. So far, I have spoken at three of them. I have travelled to Eton to speak to the Political Society; it is, I suppose a question of upbringing, but I felt I had last arrived. The invitation to perform in that misty valley and in the room where M. R. James had breakfasted, gave me great pleasure. As a tribute both to A. J. Balfour and Harold Macmillan, I tucked the ends of my black tie carefully beneath the wings of my collar. I bet they don't do that in Chingford. I dined with the Provost and his wife and, emboldened by the college claret, spoke for an hour. Ian Gilmour had warned me the night before, that my audience would be at least as alarming and certainly cleverer than the House of Commons. He was right on the second count. I looked for the young Widmerpool and it was not long before I found him.

I have been to Rugby, which must be the dullest small town in England, to speak to the Tawney Society, which seemed to be under the impression I was to talk about the sex life of Dr Arnold. I cannot think what gave them that idea. It put me in some difficulty. And Bradfield, where the sixth form is harangued every Saturday morning during the winter and spring terms by a glittering assortment who, tempted by a cheque for a hundred pounds, drop everything and make for the Berkshire Hills. Every April the school publishes the marks awarded by the boys and girls to their guests. I came fifth out of sixteen, one ahead of Richard Ingrams but behind a parson. At Rugby a housemaster and I discussed the change that came over the public schools in the sixties, an act of liberation. 'There are good schools and there are happy schools,' I was told. 'I am afraid that Rugby is becoming a happy school.'

But all roads lead to Westminster. Sooner or later, drained of healing power, we return to its gothic spires, nodding a greeting towards the Whips, saying 'hello' to the girls of the lobby, congratulating our friends and cutting our enemies. And then into the Members' Dining Room in search of congenial company to go with the cold roast beef. We gossip like scullery maids only to be interrupted at long last by the ringing of bells. Summoned like so many Betjemans, we shuffle off to do our duty and vote for whatever it is our masters have managed to slip into the manifesto.

9   *The Rhubarb and the Rubbish*

At the time of year when the leaves begin to turn, politicians of all parties abandon their buckets and spades and take tickets for seaside resorts out of season. October is for some the cruellest month; for others, the tillers in the political vineyard, who have spent the year addressing either their friends or envelopes, it is the best of times when the party leaders present themselves for exhortation, rebuke and chastisement.

I have been going to Conservative Party Conferences for years, although it is only recently that I have been paid by newspapers and magazines to do so. Their subvention is welcome, but it has meant a pilgrimage from one Party Conference to another, from Buxton to Bournemouth by way of Blackpool and Brighton. Dip beneath the surface similarities, the rhubarb and the rubbish, and there are differences: the Social Democrats seem to attract the examination-taking classes, *Guardian* readers with yellow Volvos and two children, one of whom suffers from dyslexia; the Liberals are a blend of the old middle classes and the bearded practitioners of 'community politics' whereby broken paving stones acquire a curious doctrinal significance; the Labour Party is certainly not a band of brothers; and the Conservative Conference has, under Mrs Thatcher's populist leadership, become, to all intents and purposes, a working class festival.

Whatever its composition, the Party Conference is no place for a sensitive backbencher. The Member of Parliament is not at his best at Brighton or Blackpool. If he is called on to speak, he is liable to say things like, 'Mr Chairman, far too many of our policemen are being shot', or 'What our young people want is a piece of blue sky.' On the conference floor

he moves in stately convoy escorted by members of his constituency party anxious lest he escape them. In the corridors on the way to a lunch given by Mr Brian Walden, he will greet colleagues whom at Westminster he will go to any lengths to avoid. If he is newly-elected he will have pinned, next to his inner wheel, a badge which reads 'I love Maggie', a box of which gathers dust in his constituency office. His face will be fixed into a central-lobby smile, combining gratitude towards those to whom he owes everything with a touch of resolution. He has his finger on the pulse of the Nation.

In recent years, I have striven to achieve invisibility. The Member is under pressure to attend; twenty years ago, if he came at all it was for a day during which he would lunch or dine with the representatives from his constituency; today he is one of the boys. He will take tea with people whose names he cannot quite remember, and he will be invited to address the Wallasey Young Conservatives on his only free Friday in November. 'We had hoped for Norman Tebbit but we should be delighted . . .' Sooner or later he is driven back into the hall.

I derive some comfort from the performances of my peers, for each debate is wound up by the appropriate Minister (or Shadow). Mr John Selwyn Gummer, the Party Chairman, looking like a crystallised choirboy, the scourge of our Bishops about whom there is still something faintly risible. Mr Norman Fowler, once of *The Times*, who never seems to attract the attention he deserves, and Mr Patrick Jenkin who most certainly does. Mr Nigel Lawson, who frankly does not give a damn. Sir Keith Joseph, wearing one black and one brown shoe, writhing in self-abasement, and Lord Whitelaw, the fastest gun in the North, whose bluff exterior conceals the softest of centres. But they are only the hors d'œuvre, taken, as it were, from the revolving trolley of political fortune; the main course consists of the annual duel between Michael Heseltine and Norman Tebbit who lock arms to see who can claim the longest and most rapturous applause.

Unless Mrs Thatcher were to go under a bus, she will be succeeded in a few years time as leader of the Conservative Party by either Heseltine or Tebbit. Or, to put it another way, this is what the rivals confidently expect. I would not discount the chances of either John Biffen or Peter Walker. But given the premise on which they perform, Michael and Norman's speeches are judged accordingly. Heseltine has made himself into an orator of the traditional sort, devoting, so it is claimed, many months to the preparation of his speech, which to the amusement of the cognoscenti, can range well beyond the remit of his departmental responsibility. Tebbit's style is much more relaxed.

Michael Heseltine, who is no 'Thatcherite', does, to his credit, try to lift his audience away from their immediate concerns and point them in the direction of the real world. He talks about unemployment, social deprivation and the fate of our inner cities; as Secretary of State for Defence his scope is more limited, restricted to the demolition of the case for unilateral nuclear disarmament, and the defence of Trident. In 1984 he slipped into bathos, declaiming, in hushed tones, a section of his speech about D-Day which must have been the work of Sir Arthur Bryant. He should strive for a lighter touch and more humour.

Norman Tebbit has the advantage of having his prejudices in common with those of the Conservative Party's rank and file. He is the embodiment of the party's 'gothic revival'. He can combine a fundamentalist approach with an attractively self-deprecatory humour which serves to reinforce his message. In 1984, before he was so grievously injured by the Brighton bomb, his speech was the more successful of the two. Whereas Michael Heseltine can bring the conference to its feet, Norman Tebbit can bring it to its knees.

It was, of course, A. J. Balfour who said that he would sooner take advice from his valet than from the Conservative Conference, and I have little doubt that today Margaret would never dream of saying as much. The Tory Party Conference is a rally, a festival of some light and a little heat during which note is taken of the concerns of the party faithful (in the past, Rhodesia: today, crime and punishment) but whose proper purpose is to enthuse. Whatever else can be said for or against the Conservative Party, it has demonstrated a mastery of the techniques of political public relations. The Thatcher Government is in tune as never before with the bulk of its party activists.

It is the fact that Tories rally and do not confer that explains why a Conservative Party Conference is 'rigged' in a more obvious way than are the others. Motions for debate are carefully chosen from the many hundreds that are submitted by 650 constituency associations so as to suit the convenience of the leadership. Sometimes thorny points cannot simply be evaded; if the rank and file feel strongly about capital punishment for terrorist offences, a subject which is likely to feature even more prominently at future Party Conferences, then it must be debated, the Home Secretary of the day being called upon to make the Government's case. A favourite device when times are bad, is to hold a debate adversely critical of the Government's public relations, something which the simpler Conservative will blame for the unpalatability of Government policies. The party leadership conspire with the anxious in order that morale may be restored by the undertaking to take more care about the 'presentation' of the party's policies. After all, most Conservatives believe in what a Conservative Government is doing; the fact that others may not can best be explained, or cauterised, by finding fault with the party's rainmakers who 'have not been getting our message across'. The irony is, of course, that they have been only too successful in doing precisely that.

The Chairman of the Conference is advised as to who to call to speak. Notorious troublemakers are left to fume in their seats, while a succession of worthy young men and women are invited in turn to take their place at the rostrum. There is invariably a conference 'high spot', in which, for example, a black, pregnant Young Conservative trades unionist from Brixton condemns socialism and all its works to ecstatic applause. In 1984 the Tory Party in conference was obliged to listen to an attack mounted against the Established Church by a bearded Sikh, and loved every minute of it. What would the great Lord Salisbury have made of it?

I have no objection to the rigging of the Conference. The alternative, sending a mandated platform back to Westminster with a flea in its ear, might well be worse; but it does blunt the attempts of those who have doubts about the Government's economic policy, and in particular, its failure to halt the rise in the number of people out of work, to draw public and party attention to their doubts. Dissent has to be kept for meetings on the fringe.

The growth of fringe meetings is something we have pinched from our rivals. The Tories can have up to sixty meetings arranged, meetings at which such luminaries as Mr Teddy Taylor, Dr Rhodes Boyson and Mr George Gardiner offer the forces of their minds freely to the Nation: the Conservative Group for Homosexual Equality in 1983 advertised a talk on 'Homosexuality, Security and Conservatism' which must have teased the two-bottle squires, while prominent 'wets', who have been moving from one safe house to another, break cover at a meeting of the Tory Reform Group, the most suitable 'drop' for coded messages of dissent. There is something for everyone.

In the late forties, when I first travelled north to Blackpool from Euston, pulled by a Stanier Pacific locomotive, we

THIS IS THE 'WETS HOLE'
WHERE FRANCIS PYM
STAYS DURING CONFERENCE.

would spend our evenings on the floor. A party of
Hampstead Young Conservatives, under the stern and
unbending eye of Geoffrey Finsberg, would have had its
expenses paid by the local party; our days would be spent
listening respectfully to Captain Macmillan and Mr Harry
Crookshank; our nights, gliding across the floor of the Winter

Gardens to a twelve-piece band. Bold spirits would be called upon to address the conference ('We want 300,000 houses a year . . .'). I can remember the young Nicholas Scott, a slim William van Straubenzee, an earnest Peter Walker, while bolder spirits still would pursue the trim secretaries of Midlands YC branches back to their boarding houses. Were we not committed to 'setting the people free'?

In those days, as in these, the Party Conference had something in common with the Proms, a thousand performances leading inevitably to the Last Night. On the Friday evening, Mr Winston Churchill would fly into Lytham St Anne's like the Lord God of Hosts, holding himself in readiness for the Leader's Speech which was the climax of the Conference. He would read us his speech, peering occasionally into the lights across the top of his half-spectacles. This was the Churchill not of 1910 but of 1940, the great opportunist who had found himself the leader of the other party.

Anthony Eden did his best to jolly us along with his dapper dress and 'Chips' Channon drawl. Harold Macmillan was never at his best; I suspect he found the whole business as ridiculous as it was tiresome. Sir Alec would address the Conference as if it were a County Agricultural Show. Ted Heath's speeches would never really come off; it is only recently that he has learnt to make us laugh. But Mrs Thatcher has come into her own. She is at her happiest beside the seaside, in front of 'her own'.

Since the days of Ted Heath's predominance, the party leader has, in a gesture towards party democracy, joined us at the start of the proceedings. She now sits on the platform, her comings and goings, attention and inattention, made much of by the political commentators. She tends to applaud any reference favourable to hanging. But her presence serves to trail her own performance, which now takes place on Friday afternoon, a time best calculated to capture the headlines in Saturday's, Sunday's and Monday's press.

To be truthful, I do not attend. The highlights of her speech will feature in every television news bulletin, and the salient points in all the newspapers. And Prime Ministerial speeches are rather like German wines, that is with reference not to the shape of the bottle but to the nature of the grape, for it is the authorship of the first draft that matters. Mrs Thatcher's speeches have not been the same since Chris Patten stopped writing them. But I have a good idea what the occasion is like.

Imagine an audience of several thousand Conservatives, all of whom have lunched well. They will have been warmed up first by Kenny Everett and then by Dame Vera Lynn singing 'The White Cliffs of Dover'. Mrs Thatcher will then be carried on to a pale-blue stage (the advice of Saatchi and Saatchi) on a throne on poles carried at its four quarters by Mr Gordon Reece, Lord McAlpine, John Selwyn Gummer and Sir Alfred Sherman. She will take her seat before the podium, an arc of acolytes around her head like cherubim about the risen Lord. Her speech will be brought in on a salver carried by Mr Bernard Ingham. After an introduction by the Chairman which contains some extraordinary historical parallels, she will stand and deliver. The Nation will be told to pull up its socks.

After four days of huffing and puffing, the Tories make for the London road, the representatives happy but tired, cheered by their proximity to the great. The party's leaders will heave sighs of relief. Deft hands will wrap them into tartan travelling rugs and the big black Rovers will make silently for the motorway. 'Thank God that's all over.'

In the autumn of 1983, I wrote a series of articles for Russell Twisk's *Listener* about the four major Party Conferences. With his kind permission I reproduce them here as an indication of the varying degrees of horror which each party inflicts on its faithful.

Plenty of nut cutlet but very little rhubarb

Gill Day

I have been led into temptation. I received a telephone call from the Editor of *The Listener* inviting me to leave my study in order to journey to Manchester where the Social Democrats would be in conference. As a Conservative I have my doubts about our regime, but I am an old conference hand — a thousand ages in my sight are like an evening gone — and I have lost count of the times I have travelled to some seaside resort out of season to herald the break of yet another new dawn; but never in Manchester.

And it meant breaking my routine, for I am of a contemplative nature and happiest seated at my desk surrounded by my treasures: a Staffordshire portrait bust of Mr Cecil Parkinson, a butt of Mrs Thatcher's cigar and my signed photograph of Sir Alfred Sherman. I was also busily engaged in reviewing Sir Geoffrey Howe's autobiography (*Sheep's Clothing*, The Morpheus Press). Should I abandon all this for the rigours of Manchester and the charms of Mrs Shirley Williams?

I have only visited Manchester twice before, each time for a day, to appear on one of Granada's noisier programmes, and I did not know what to expect. Were Mancunians really a race of earnest, bespectacled schoolmasters in khaki shorts dedicated to keeping open the Pennine Way? I have lunched with the *Guardian* and suffered at the school where Neville Cardus taught cricket, but I have never until this week spent a night in that great city. I am left with three impressions: it was wet and windy; its architecture consists of 19th- and 20th-century warehouses; and it has the best Chinese restaurant this side of Kowloon. I refer to the Yang Sing, of 17 George Street (061-236 2200), which has just been awarded *The Good Food Guide's* award as 'the Chinese restaurant of the year'. It has its own pestle and mortar. I dined there twice on a selection of Dim Sum: fried crabmeat balls, paper-wrapped prawns and steamed chicken and mushrooms. They were delicious. As I ate, the basement filled up with prosper-

97

ous Social Democrats and their pretty wives who had come to Manchester so as to put the troubles of Dartington far behind them.

The Social Democrats belong clearly to the Volvo-owning classes. The conference, which was small enough to be held at the University of Salford, hitherto famous for its collection of Lowrys, was a decorous affair in which textual criticism was muted and the speakers well spoken and brisk without any displays of temper. The great and the good sat on the platform in front of a large Dutch flag, the significance of which escaped me, while Shirley Williams, who was thrillingly stern but kind, kept order. What I really missed was the show and the spite.

At Tory conferences we are bored by the Mayor, take the Almighty into our confidence, and are presided over by some amiable old buffer whose cheerful incompetence is invariably rewarded with a knighthood. It was not like that at Salford. There was no sign of the Revd Nick Stacey (or God), although Mr Paul Masson, who had flown in from California, was in attendance. It was a little smug: an atmosphere of brown rice, Cabernet Sauvignon and the *Ham and High;* although points were made rationally, rhetoric cut to the bone and rhubarb largely absent. That is not at all what I am used to.

The delegates (or are they representatives?) reminded me of

a saying of Verlaine: *'Pas de couleur, rien que la nuance'.* It was all so genteel. The Tory Party conference has largely become a working-class festival, where those who have rallied to Mrs Thatcher's populist standard come in order to rail against the trade union movement, and call for less crime and more punishment. Each year a prominent Tory is tossed from the platform into the crowd, a necessary sacrifice for the party's good. A fate that did not befall Mr Brocklebank-Fowler at Salford.

Perhaps I am being unfair? I have come to regard the Tory conference as an entertainment where obscure MPs with dull wives and a cat called Alderman Roberts mount the rostrum and reveal a set of prejudices to which previously only their constituents have been privy. Black, working-class, female Young Conservatives ('and another little one on the way') attack socialism to a standing ovation, while Rotarians, the victims of a thousand lunches, make bad jokes about Roy Jenkins and his claret. At Salford there were no master butchers, just a sad absence of vulgarity, a tendency to treat politics as if it were a rational activity, a courtesy toward friend and foe which bodes ill for the health of the body politic. Do they intend to rob me of all my pleasures?

Shirley Williams has retained one irritating habit from her past: the neglect of the definite article. She refers not to *the* conference but to 'conference' (do left-wing Jews refer to 'Ark of Covenant'?), but it is a custom which has even spread to Mrs T.'s Conservative Party. It was hard to tell the media people from the rank and file, and the word 'civilised' was, unlike at a Tory conference, rarely used as a term of abuse. One speaker, emboldened by a light lunch, wondered if the SDP might earn the title 'the hyenas of politics'. I can set his fears at rest. Everyone seemed short of tongue and long in temper, making Salford quite unlike Matthew Arnold's 'Dover Beach' 'where ignorant armies clash by night', which can typify activities elsewhere.

I suspect that the Social Democrats will long remain *in statu pupillari*. The ambitions of General Galtieri (who is to travel to Blackpool next month to receive his award for services to the Conservative Party), the nature of the electoral system and the shrewdness of the Cabinet who pressed for a June election against the strong opposition of the Prime Minister herself have placed Mrs Thatcher in the happy position of a Baldwin or a Chamberlain: able to take advantage at successive general elections of a divided Opposition. The Labour Party under Kinnock and Meacher will travel on a dream ticket of the Tories' printing, as the erosion of the Labour vote continues, but more slowly than before. The Alliance will compete for the middle-class vote with Mrs Thatcher's New Model Conservatism, which will, in its turn, strengthen its hold upon the working-class vote. Attractive as it is, I cannot see the SDP breaking the mould.

There is still something of the Amateur Night about it. Its appeal has been almost exclusively to the Left, and Christopher Brocklebank-Fowler remains the only Tory MP to have crossed the floor. The Tory 'wets', who have not won a major battle, are still unwilling to concede defeat, being naturally reluctant to abandon their party to an uncongenial blend of Samuel Smiles and Pierre Poujade. Mrs Thatcher, who leads her party from the Right, finds her natural constituency upon the back benches, and thus will be impossible to shift. Events may conspire against her, but the more realistic among the 'old' Tories are looking beyond Mrs T. to her successor. In the meantime, we will do all we can to soften the asperities.

While I ate my lunch in the sixth-floor canteen (yoghurt and a nut cutlet), a journalist from one of the popular papers approached and asked when I would join the SDP. I said I had no intention of doing so. I would resist the temptation. I have been a Tory for a long time; and, anyway, what on earth would our great party do without me?

Julian Critchley is still Conservative MP for Aldershot.

Beards, badges, and the lost innocence of wheatgerm

No sooner had I returned, drained of healing power, from the SDP conference in Salford than I found myself boarding a Great Northern Railway express from King's Cross bound for Harrogate and the Liberals. My life, which has hitherto been a sheltered one, was about to be subjected to yet another cultural shock. I had time only to acknowledge several letters from grateful constituents and to respond to an invitation from Chairman Gummer to put my ideas for a new coat of arms for our great party upon 'one side of a piece of paper'. (I did so: a Range Rover, an abacus and a scold's bridle.) More seriously, I had also to abandon my task of correcting the proofs of Mr Nigel Lawson's autobiography *(Mrs Portnoy's Complaint,* Chutzpah and Chutzpah).

I should confess that I dragged my feet. En route I called on Mrs Phyllis White, who is better known as P. D. James, the detective story writer, in order to interview her for the *Illustrated London News,* a venerable journal that sells to expatriates, Sir Arthur Bryant and to all those who suffer from dental decay. She is a charmer. She told me that her father had made it his rule that if he had to vote, he would do so for the 'Gentlemen's party'; I observed that, were he in a position to do so today, he would find himself somewhat confused.

As a parting gift, P. D. James gave me an inscribed copy of her book *Innocent Blood;* what better to take with me to a Liberal conference?

At York, I broke my journey to visit the National Railway Museum, where a collection of gleaming steam-engines stand in a circle to be admired by railway buffs and polished by their neglected wives. There were locomotives from all the old railway companies: 2-8-0s from the Great Western; 4-4-0s from the London and South Western and an 0-4-2T from the Great Eastern. I inquired of an attendant whether there was an engine called 'Gladstone'. I was told that it was no longer on display. Sadly, I walked back to the station and boarded a North Eastern stopping train for Harrogate.

I had heard something of the

misbehaviour of the Young Liberals, and expected perhaps a pall of smoke to be hanging over the town. Had Harrogate been put to the torch? But the town seemed peaceful enough, a kind of northern Cheltenham, built of a blacker stone, over which floated, like some pre-1914 Cunarder, the vast bulk of the Hotel Majestic. Blue-haired widows of the sort whose daughters had been seduced by Joe Lampton sipped their Earl Grey in genteel cafés and waited for their escorts, retired majors, honed in body and mind by hours spent upon the golf course, whose task it was to convoy them safely back to their villas, past the spot where a small bunch of flowers marked the final meeting of minds between the Young Liberals and Lady Olga Maitland, saint and martyr.

Having checked in at the Old Swan, and taken some refreshment, I set out down mean streets for the conference itself, which was being held, so I was told, in a brand-new conference centre. I saw a sign which read 'To the Northern Antiques Fair', and headed resolutely in its direction. Could those willowy young men with soft white hands and Kensington accents really be the dreaded Young Liberals? From one of them I bought a Liverpool creamer, *circa* 1790, on which were inscribed the words 'Agriculture, Commerce and Freedom of the Seas', which is, as slogans go, not at all bad. Clutching my purchase,

I was pointed in the direction of the Liberal conference, a forum where, I was told, every object really was more than a hundred years old.

It was, I should confess, a shock. The hall was filled with dust, hoarse cries and the sound of wooden sword clashing upon wooden sword, for all the world as if the Sealed Knot — which is, as *Listener* readers will know, a body in which the dotty dress up in the costumes either of the Roundheads or the Cavaliers (save for their Hush Puppies) and prance about reliving the Battle of Edgehill — had been invited to perform. I withdrew into the foyer and admired the stalls, which ranged from photographs of the appallingly scarred victims of Hiroshima to 'specially treated hyacinths for early forcing'. I bought some fudge and a badge which read 'Denis Thatcher needs help', which will come in handy when I reach Blackpool.

Later, I strolled to the Cairns in order to attend, at the invitation of Mr Alan Beith, the party's Chief Whip, a meeting of the ALC, or the Association of Liberal Councillors, which was to be addressed by two of the party's rising stars: Mr Michael Meadowcroft and Mr Paddy Ashdown; the victors respectively of Leeds and Yeovil. The Liberals set great store on what they call 'community politics', in which holes in the road assume a curious doctrinal importance. Others, not so impressed, have described this activity as 'mindless' and 'instant compassion'. Nevertheless, it has had its successes, drains being converted to votes, particularly where the sitting MP has not been up to much.

Michael Meadowcroft was chatty and engaging, the very best sort of school-teacher, but he told me nothing I did not already know; Mr Ashdown, on the other hand, who was no less chatty and engaging, enunciated 'Ashdown's Law', which is that anyone who owns a Jack Russell terrier is a Liberal supporter. My neighbour, who had been taking notes throughout the meeting, solemnly added this piece of information to the rest. I was still pondering this truth when my cover was blown by Mr Stephen Ross, and I was given the bum's rush, despite my shrill protests to the effect that I, too, was the owner of a Jack Russell. (*This is true; his name is Humphrey, and he has a very nice nature — Ed.*)

Shaken by the indignity of it all, I crossed the Rippon Road to a restaurant called Number Six (Harrogate 502908), where I dined with Mr Peter Riddell, who writes about politics for the *Financial Times*. We comforted ourselves with grouse, for I am, after all, a High Tory, and shared a bottle of Bonnes Mares, Comte Georges de Vogüé, 1970, which put me in a better temper. We went on to discuss the Young Liberals, who were, at that time, happily engaged in setting fire to another part of the town.

They all wear uniform: denim jackets, open-necked shirts and shoes without socks. Beneath their beards they carry across their chests rows of badges, each espousing some frightful cause. Every morning they present themselves to the world with self-conscious art, daily remaking themselves in their own image. They have long lost the innocence of wheatgerm, being filled with the barely suppressed anger of those who have grabbed for themselves enough privilege to know just how little privilege they will achieve. Judging by the noise they make, they are anti-American and pro-Soviet, views which are made worse by the self-righteousness and bad manners with which they are expressed. What a trial they must be to the good doctor Owen.

I did not miss the Leader's speech. Over the years I have witnessed the performances of the great, from Winston Churchill (the real one) to the Great She Elephant herself. The finale at Harrogate was a sad disappointment. There was no warm-up by Billy Connolly, no rendering of 'Scotland the Brave' by Miss Moira Anderson, and Mr Steel's knees remained decently hidden beneath Bradford cloth. So, too, did most of his ideas.

Julian Critchley is the Conservative MP for Aldershot.

Popcorn, ale from cans and a display of brotherly love

I returned from the Sack of Harrogate — all those burnt-out Triumph Sodomites, the smashed Doulton and ruptured cocktail cabinets — to a heavy post-bag. And my Jack Russell had become insufferably vain, having developed a taste for publicity. There was a communication from Lady Olga Maitland's solicitors suggesting an agreement whereby if I undertook not to mention their client in any of the papers in which I write, she would not include me in her column in the *Sunday Express*, and a postcard from Queretaro in Mexico with the message 'Wish you were here', signed 'Alfred'. Now, who could that be?

But there was one envelope which contained only a small square of paper, the size of a lump of sugar, on which had been drawn in pencil a black spot. This was sinister. Naturally, I wondered who was responsible. The literary allusion would exclude the bulk of Conservative MPs, most of whom believe that Robert Louis Stevenson was responsible for inventing the steam-engine.

Could it have been Chairman Gummer? I rang his secretary at Conservative Central Office, a charming girl called Fiona, who sounded handsome. She said that it was unlikely to have been the Chairman as he would have included a leaflet from the Church Missionary Society. Had I thought of trying Mr Nigel Lawson?

I did not relish the prospect of telephoning the Cabinet, from the Prime Minister's Office downwards, remembering Mr Harold Macmillan's dictum, delivered at a recently held meeting of the Conservative Philosophy Group under the chairmanship of Lord Everett of Wembley, that the Government consisted of 'a brilliant tyrant, surrounded by mediocrities'. Instead, I began to worry about the Labour Party, and how best to get to Brighton, in order to report for *Listener* readers the outcome of the big fight between Neil Kinnock of Bedwellty and Roy Hattersley of Birmingham, Sparkbrook.

Taking a leaf out of Chesterton, I travelled to Brighton by way of Newcastle, in order to appear on *Friday Live*, a late-night programme, which is the flagship of

103

Tyne-Tees Television. It consisted of a line of pundits who had been asked to discuss the nature of opposition (Mr Michael Fallon, the Tory MP for Darlington, had been invited by mistake: it was believed by the producer that he was as 'wet' as I am), and a rabble of protesters, reflecting every grievance known to man, who spent the last half of the programme crying 'diabolical liberty'. Why is it that the Left cannot employ the word 'liberty' without this tiresome prefix? Tucked away beneath the banners were three savants, Mr Michael White, who makes jokes about MPs for the *Guardian*, Mr Paul Johnson, who is employed as a hired gun by the *Daily Mail*, and Mr Ludovic Kennedy, who had broken his journey from Edinburgh to see how the other half lives.

It was a dog's breakfast. Mr Joe Ashton savaged the Labour Party's policies, Mr Ken Livingstone put in a word in defence of his livelihood, while Mr Bob Clay, the newly elected Labour MP for Sunderland, lustred in pink, was not prepared to blame the party for its defeats, but rather the people, who were, it seemed, incapable of recognising a good thing when they saw one. It was a taste of what was to come at Brighton.

Miss Gillian Reynolds, who is known as the 'Iron Lady of Tyne and Wear', was in the chair. 'Did you,' she said, coming to me, 'refer to Mrs Thatcher in *The Listener* as "the Great She Elephant"?' Wishing to ingratiate myself with both ladies, I explained that in Swaziland the term is one of respect, even of admiration, being reserved for the local equivalent of the Queen Mother. But to no avail; my compliment was all over the Sunday papers, and, once again, I am in hot water. My gently satirical style should not be permitted to fall into the hands of brutal and insensitive hacks.

I arrived at Brighton, travelling on a dream ticket, late the next morning in need of rest and recuperation. I went to English's for lunch, six oysters and a bottle of beer, and spent the afternoon looking at the antique shops in the Lanes, which were disappointing, and visiting the museum where there is a splendid collection of 18th- and 19th-century ceramics.

The next morning I strolled along the promenade as far as the Metropole, to attend a fringe meeting. Far out to sea loomed the grey outline of a great warship; could it be the USS *New Jersey?* The members of Labour Solidarity had gathered in the Clarendon Room, to listen to home truths from Mr Peter Shore and Mr Roy Hattersley, truths that were warmly received by what might be called the better end of the Labour Party. After a light lunch I blew 50 pence, the entrance fee charged to attend a meeting of the Campaign for Labour Democracy, held in the splendour of the Corn Exchange.

We were harangued by Mr Eric Clarke of the Scottish NUM, whose accent was so thick that, mercifully, much of what he had to say was lost; and by a Mr Deal of the Fire Brigade, Frankly, I was horrified; each assertion — for example that they were speaking in the name of the working class (surely Mrs T. has pinched most of them?) — being greeted with sustained applause. It was a little like Open Day at the Salpêtrière, but without the good offices of Professor Charcot. I must say, I shall look at Norman Tebbit in a new light. Indeed, I was so shocked I felt obliged to return to my modest hotel and put my feet up.

At 5.30, ignoring some old-fashioned looks, I took my place high up in the gods, to witness what the press had once billed as 'the fight of the century'. Could Neil Kinnock, the engaging Welsh lightweight with a silver tongue, sponsored by Gillette, the makers of the Dry Look, give weight away to his challenger, Roy Hattersley, sponsored by *The Listener*, the *Guardian* and *Punch*, known to those of his enemies who have read his recently published autobiography as the 'Immaculate Misconception'? At ringside, large men in purple pinstriped suits engaged in conversation blonde ladies who were dead ringers for Miss Barbara Windsor, while the plebs, in the cheaper seats, placed their bets, drank pale ale from cans and munched popcorn. Fraternal greetings were brought by Mr Mickey Duff.

As is now well known, the Welsh Wizard won by a mile, taking every round by a wide margin, picking up the verdicts of all three judges and the referee, four venerable gentlemen wearing dark glasses and carrying white sticks. Shrill cries of 'we wuz robbed' from those of the delegates who wore ties obliged the stewards to compensate Roy with the Deputy Leadership belt on the presentation of which both fighters fell upon each others' shoulders in an unconvincing display of brotherly love. In Saturday's *Daily Telegraph* there was the sad story of a Mrs Maureen Gledhill, who thought she had bought a bargain when she acquired an abstract painting for £70; it was only later that she discovered that it had been painted by a duck. Could the same thing have happened to the Labour Party?

In three weeks I have dined with the SDP, sensible chaps with two wives, a country cottage and three children, one of whom suffers from dyslexia, taken breakfast with the Liberals and supped with the People's Party. I have now to travel north to attend the Tory conference in Blackpool. I hereby promise to make no jokes at the expense of Our Great Leader, an assurance which may not be enough to avoid the need of my taking desperate measures, such as being smuggled into the Winter Gardens rolled up in a rug. In the meantime, I am going to The Hague to worry about cruise and Pershing. Should I apply for political asylum?

Julian Critchley is the Conservative MP for Aldershot.

I arrived at Blackpool station, lugging my suitcase and typewriter. As I left the platform an aircraft flew overhead trailing a banner which read 'Maggie rules . . . OK?' I looked heavenwards and promptly tore a muscle in my hip. I was taken by taxi to my £9 a day digs, where I lay prostrate for three days, listening to the proceedings on the radio. I never set foot at the conference. Nor did I make mention of Cecil Parkinson over whose *affaire de coeur* the world made such a fuss. I 'killed off' Sir Alfred Sherman instead.

Julian Critchley: With his own folk at Blackpool

Pork pies, milk stout and mutton dressed as lamb

I was seen off from Euston Station, en route for the Conservative conference at Blackpool, by none other than the Editor of *The Listener*, Mr Russell Twisk himself.

Did I glimpse a manly tear in his eye as the good fellow bade me farewell? He pressed comforts upon me: a packet of cheese sandwiches left over from the meeting of the General Advisory Committee of the BBC, and an illustrated book about elephants by Sir David Attenborough. It was civil of him.

Having been mugged by a gentleman from the *Sunday Telegraph*, I had taken the precaution of visiting a West End firm of theatrical costumiers. Should I travel north on the conference special disguised as a Polish cavalry officer, *circa* 1939,

or as a bishop? I chose the latter, as my ecclesiastical clobber would serve to protect me from every predator, save Chairman Gummer.

The journey was uneventful enough. Rival bands of Young Conservatives ranged the length of the train searching either for Mr Matthew Parris or Mr Harvey Proctor, Rotarians recited their rules over lunch, and the ticket-collector was pressed into selling raffle tickets. The noise from the buffet car was particularly tiresome: breaking glass, the sound of triumphal laughter and the frequent rendering of unfamiliar, martial-sounding songs. It was just like the good old days, when, uncorrupted by my peers, I would travel to Blackpool in the company of Mr Ernest Marples.

I delayed leaving the train at

Blackpool when something caught my eye. I thought for a moment it was porters larking with the mails, but a small ceremony seemed to be taking place. A group of the prominenti, what Miss Jean Brodie would have described as the *crème de la crème* of our great party, had assembled on the platform as a welcoming committee.

Chairman Gummer seemed to be in charge. A silver-haired, distinguished-looking military figure, somewhat shrunken in appearance and dressed in what must have been the Latin-American equivalent of a demob suit, climbed unsteadily down from the buffet. He was embraced by Mr Ian Gow (I caught the name 'Leopoldo'), and introduced to the waiting committee. Lord Thomas, Sir Ronald Millar, whose quips have enlivened many a prime ministerial address, Mr 'Buster' Mottram, whose Conservative Political Centre lecture on the future of race relations (*Love-All?* CPC Publications) was eagerly anticipated, and Mr Teddy Taylor were, in turn, introduced to the General, who had come, as forecast in *The Listener*, to receive in person the first annual Galtieri Award for services to the Conservative Party. The moving ceremony was concluded by the singing, at the bidding of Chairman Gummer, of the first verse of 'Jesus Wants Me for a Sunbeam'. The General was then bundled into one of Syd's Taxis in the company of another rough-looking Scot. Could it have been Sir John Junor?

I made my way to my very modest hotel (£9 a day), and changed into something more comfortable. Over a gammon steak and pineapple I scrutinised the list of delights contained in the conference programme of events. There was an *embarras du choix*. I might have danced the night away at the Winter Gardens to the music of the Poisonous Acolytes at the Young Conservative Ball, enveloped in clouds of blue tulle, but I thought better of all that mutton dressed as lamb. I could have paid a visit to the North Pier and seen a performance of *Fiddler on the Roof*, but I had had enough of Nigel Lawson. Finally, there was the Bow Group cocktail party at the Imperial Hotel, but the prospect of all those 16-year-old merchant bankers in Gummer glasses, talking about the money supply and urging on me the need for a resolute approach, failed to attract.

Although I have never really understood the Conservative Party, I have been hugely entertained by it. It is a tribe in which loyalty is given to the Leader (hence my 'Great She Elephant'), whose most active members assemble yearly at a seaside resort out of season to let off steam. A minority wishes to confer; that is, to push the leadership in directions which it might find uncongenial, e.g. the expulsion of black Britons; the majority, however, travel in order to enjoy themselves, to celebrate past triumphs, offer generalised support and rub shoulders with the great. It is not so much a conference, more a festival, the climax of which is the Leader's speech on the Friday afternoon.

I rose late and read the northern editions of the papers, but I set out for the Winter Gardens in good time, travelling by a circuitous route and stopping for a light lunch at Piggies (Blackpool 20803) in Deansgate Street, where I ate a sustaining pork pie just like my mother used to make and drank a glass of milk stout. The café was packed with hungry Tories eating for two, because three days at a party conference can be debilitating.

All gas and gaiters, I hurried to take my seat at the back of the hall, tucked discreetly behind a pillar. I might have been mistaken for the Bishop of Bath and Wells. I was immediately aware of what might be called 'an atmosphere'. Clearly something momentous had happened, the nature of which I was not aware. Party agents were ashen-faced, whispering together in the aisles, hearty girls who could take Michael Heseltine in their stride were being comforted by older women, and George Gardiner had given way to tears. I inquired of my neighbour the cause of this undoubted consternation. 'Haven't you heard,' she said sternly, 'Sir Alfred Sherman has passed on.'

Readers of *The Listener* can imagine how I felt. And it had happened at the hands of savages! Apparently he had been shot in the course of some doctrinal dispute in the remote Mexican town of Q————, and had been buried in the Emperor Maximilian's grave. Naturally, the arrangements for the Prime Minister's rally had hurriedly to be altered. Lord Everett of Wembley was not permitted to warm up the crowd in advance of The Speech, despite his willingness to do so wearing a black tie, while Dame Vera Lynn, who had been asked to sing 'The White Cliffs of Dover', had to be unceremoniously stood down. On the arrival of Mrs Thatcher, the conference stood for a minute's silence. I noticed the General, supported on either side by a Vice-Chairman of the party organisation, clutching his award, which was a copy of *Margaret Thatcher, Wife, Mother and Politician* by Penny Junor. It was in this way that we mourned the passing of the Great Mahout.

What more can I say? If, in the 19th century, religion was described as 'morality tinged with emotion', a Thatcher speech is quite the reverse. I shall discuss Thatcherism and the formidable Mrs T. in a future Centrepiece when I will examine two recently published books: Penny Junor's; and *The Thatcher Government* by Peter Riddell. In the last four weeks I have travelled the country, sampling the goods on offer by all four parties, guineas succeeding where wild horses would have failed to detach me from my study. Party conferences are a necessary price paid by the great; those of us who lurk upon the back benches are only bullied into attendance by our agents. Certainly, a Conservative conference is no place for a sensitive backbencher.

And what have I to show? A sheaf of cuttings and a Liverpool jug *circa* 1790. But I shall visit Anthony Oliver's shop in Church Street, Kensington, and purchase a Staffordshire figure of the Duke of Wellington, who published and was not damned. I have at times been satirical, but nothing I have attempted, however fanciful, can match the flow of events. Reality is best. As I left for Blackpool, my youngest daughter said cheerfully, 'Who are you going to offend this week, Daddy?', and I could only think of the Queen Mother.

Julian Critchley is, despite everything, still the Conservative MP for Aldershot.

10 Singing and Dancing

Members of Parliament are surrounded by temptation. We are threatened by little pink slips which the more fortunate can find in their cubby holes in the Members' Lobby, scribbled telephone messages gravely delivered by flunkies, invitations to pontificate and to perform. Our egos, already inflated by election, and by a Prime Ministerial inquiry into the well-being of our wives, are further inflated by the media, which are only too keen to persuade us into indiscretion by putting pen to paper or by appearing fleetingly on programmes such as BBC's *Newsnight*, for the most meagre of rewards. What I like best about life at the Palace of Varieties is arriving: the murmured greetings of respectful policemen, and the stately progress through cloakrooms and lavatory, pausing only to glance at the ticker-tapes, a paragraph of which is invariably scored in red by some nameless functionary marking, not as might be expected, the assassination of the Head of State of a Friendly Power, but the relegation to the Fourth Division of Mansfield Town, before emerging finally into the gothic splendour of the Members' Lobby.

The Lobby is encircled by eight plinths, seven of which support statues of former Prime Ministers (the most recent inhabitant is Major Attlee); the eighth, which is empty, is frequently occupied by St Michael Allison, Mrs Thatcher's Parliamentary Private Secretary. On a good day an attendant with medals will press into your hand currency in the shape of folded slips of paper, importuning messages from the outside world. These are pocketed, to be opened later in the tea room, to the consternation of friends and enemies.

The Members' Lobby is a place of assignation, gossip and rebuke, where Whips catch up with errant members of their flock. ('Where were you at 11.30 last Thursday night?' 'Between the thighs of an Armenian whore'), or press for payment in advance for pre-publication copies of Nigel Lawson's autobiography (*Fiddler on the Roof,* Spectator Publications). But a touch on the elbow need not be that of Mr Peter Lloyd, who is my area Whip; it might be that of Miss Margaret van Hattam of the *Financial Times* with an invitation to dine with an Irish poet, or that of Mr Julian Haviland of *The Times* in search of guidance. It could also be the lobby correspondent of the Eatanswill *Echo,* sucking the stub of his pencil and wondering when you next intend to visit the constituency. The Great, if not the Good, can be immediately recognised by the cluster of hacks about them who, notebooks in hand, stand ready to transmit their ramblings to the Nation. It has been said that it is difficult to cross the Central Lobby (which is as far as the public is permitted to come) without seeing a pretty woman; the Members' Lobby is, on the other hand, a place to escape from one's colleagues. Lobby correspondents are more discreet, but also more fun.

Having entered the Members' Lobby the MP is faced with three choices: a door which leads to the Chamber, a second to the tea room, and a third, to the real world. Most take tea, together with a rock cake of alarming density, in order to glance through their correspondence, open their telephone messages and receive congratulation upon the quality of their speeches.

The tea room is really three, the first of which contains a metal counter, cheerful foreign girls who dispense tea and toasted tea cakes, small cigars and pain-killers (free), and members of the Labour Party who, for no good reason, do not seem to penetrate any further. The next room, which has three tables, and several armchairs, is patronised by Tories among whom can be spotted members of the Whips' office in plain clothes who are under instructions to be one of the lads. In the third chamber can be found racks of newspapers, dog-eared copies of magazines and the House of Commons clerks, male and female, snatching a moment's rest. At midday the tea room serves a cheap and nasty lunch, which doubles for supper; after all night sittings, after which I feel as if I had travelled from Dieppe to Milan overnight in a third class compartment, a navvy's breakfast is served.

MPs are paid a salary of nearly £17,000 a year, a subject about which we have learnt to be wary as our masters generally wish to reduce it, our constituents tend to begrudge us every penny, and curmudgeonly journalists in newspapers like the *Sunday Express* delight in holding us up to hatred, ridicule and contempt. I make no complaint about the size of the salary, for most Members can at least double it by taking work outside. The pink slips provide pocket money.

I keep mine to the last. MPs' letters are usually about animals or abortion and come from constituents who, over the years, one has come to know and love. Then there are the invitations to lunch at the Bulgarian Embassy, to take tea with the Gas Board or to speak to the Soroptimists. A third category consists of circulars which can be tossed away unopened, and copies of dreary house magazines such as the *Thames Water Board News* and the *Concrete Quarterly*. And there are the Ministerial replies to constituents' letters, drafted by bureaucrats and signed in the small hours. Those of us who have never won promotion out of the political Fourth Division are replied to by the Parly Secs; Members of the Privy Council by Secretaries of State.

The pink slips may contain a precatory instruction to ring home, or a complete stranger ringing from Hull (usually a lunatic), or a command to get in touch immediately with a Ms Driftwood of *TV Eye, Panorama* or whatever. Now this is good news. A call, dialled in an alcove next to the Library, is put through to an earnest American, who begins, with scant ceremony, to subject one to what amounts to a *viva voce* examination on a subject of some complexity such as 'star wars'. This means that she may, if you can convince her that you know something about President Reagan's initiative, and that your preconceptions fit neatly into those of her producer, in short, if you will say what he wants you to say, invite you to take part. After an interrogation lasting twenty minutes, the conversation is cut short with the injunction 'Don't ring us'. Sometimes she rings back. It is at this stage that money is mentioned. It is a subject about which the BBC is coy; the staff of the Corporation are encouraged to act as if money were a vulgar topic, not to be discussed between the gentle. If one persists, the answer is that the fee is nothing to

do with the programme but 'a matter for accounts'. I leave it at that and wait for the arrival, weeks later, of a wad of paper which tells me to apply for a sum half the size I first thought of. ITV, on the other hand, is more generous; if the programme companies want you badly enough they are vulnerable to the game of double or quits. I was told years ago that Mr Enoch Powell never appeared on anything for a fee less than a hundred pounds, but then he believes in the market.

Ms Driftwood is to be found attached to every current affairs programme on television. An invitation to appear on Brian Walden's *Weekend World* can come from Mr Bruce Anderson, who acts as a flotilla leader to a fleet of Driftwoods but, whatever its source, it means a Friday morning visit to the Grosvenor House Hotel, where, on the seventh floor, surrounded by thirties kitsch, you are interviewed at length, a fragment of which will eventually appear on next Sunday's programme. An appearance on Channel 4's *A Week in Politics*, which does tend to be a cut above its peers, once called for a visit to an elegant house in Kensington and the gentle promptings of Mrs Roderick McFarquar, who is yet another American. Don't do it for less than a hundred pounds.

Once I travelled to Norwich to appear on Anglia's *Arena*, which was a pleasant day out. Two hours on the old Great Eastern's main line, lunch with Brian Connell and back again in time for tea. A favourite programme is *Newsnight* but it has the disadvantage of going out very late at night to an audience of insomniacs. The most prestigious of television's current affairs programmes is Robin Day's *Question Time*, but I have not been asked since its producer accused me of being rude to Ms Joan Ruddock. The programme attracts more viewers than does *Panorama*. It is a bench of Bishops presided over by the Almighty, but enjoyable, nonetheless.

Sometimes BBC2 sends a crew down to my house in Farnham and the sight of the entry of so many, some carrying equipment, does tend to impress the neighbours. Over the years, like one of Oscar Wilde's characters, I have appeared on every great programme, once.

Why do we do it? The answer must be vanity and reward. 'I saw you on the telly' is still the highest form of constituency praise, although comment is more usually reserved for one's appearance than for one's views. People rarely, if ever, actually listen to what you have to say.

I prefer radio. For the more facile there are several programmes on Radio Four on which it is fun to appear. *Quote, Unquote*, which is recorded, two episodes at a time, in a basement theatre in Lower Regent Street. And, of course, *Any Questions*, on the panel of which I am invited about once a year. The team usually meets in the foyer of the BBC building in Portland Place, where, having admired the motto in Latin ('Never apologise, never explain'), the party is driven in a black Rover to a comprehensive school in, say, Bromsgrove, where, on arrival, dinner is served. This can be fun, although I am careful to ration myself to one glass of Midlands claret. It was Sir Oswald Mosley who advised in his autobiography that no public performer should take alcohol: 'Rely', he warns, 'solely upon your own adrenalin.' I wish we could.

The chosen school is *en fête*; the Headmaster, wearing his best suit, shakes our hands, and we are led into the gymnasium which is packed with parents. A mock question to warm us up, and then we are 'on', live with nothing but our good sense to save us from indiscretion. After it is over we munch sausage rolls with the staff and then back home, down the M1 to home and bed.

Last year I was invited to appear at Pebble Mill in Birmingham and was put up the night before at a hotel in Bromsgrove, which much to my pleasure turned out to be the rectory in which A. E. Housman had lived as a child. Postcards with his picture were on sale at the foyer. The early Victorian house, with its pretty windows, had been extended à la Crossroads, but it was comfortable enough. Next morning I had breakfast in the first floor dining room of the old house; although I went to the westwards facing windows, the November mist totally obscured the view of the Clees, those 'blue, remembered hills' which the young Housman found so beguiling.

It might be fun to appear on the *News Quiz*, the preserve of Simon Hoggart whose collection of jokes in *Punch* is required reading in the Palace. Phone-ins can be entertaining but a little of vox pop goes a very long way. Five minutes on *The World at One*, if Mr Anthony Beaumont Dark is otherwise engaged, can come between the Nation and its light lunch; but if it is the Prime Minister whom you wish to impress, then a moment or two 'putting Britain first' on Radio 4's *Today* programme will provide you with an audience. An appearance on Roy Plomley's *Desert Island Discs* is most coveted of all; it is the ultimate accolade of public life, rarer by far than the knighthood, which is all too often the reward for a life of silent service. Radio 3 used to have a similar programme called *Man of Action* in which the guest was responsible not only for the records played but for the script; there was no room for the likes of Plomley. I believe Norman St John Stevas is the only Tory to have been asked to appear on it.

Breakfast television relies upon the vanity of MPs, one

commodity which will never be in short supply. We do find it difficult to say no; nevertheless the prospect of a late night call from Ms Driftwood to be followed by a restless night, an alarm call, a shave in cold water, a mini-cab and the sight of Mr David Frost, larger than life, and all on an empty stomach, does not appeal; it is a prospect beyond guineas.

And there is always the press. There are nearly as many good journalists inside as there are out. Mr Roy Hattersley was made 'Journalist of the Year', and has been writing with relish about his Yorkshire upbringings for as long as I can remember. Mr Gerald Kaufman appears to have spent his entire youth in the one shilling seats of his local Odeon, and Mr Austin Mitchell is capable of leading his squad of hand-picked American research assistants in any direction. Mr Clement Freud writes nearly as well as Elizabeth David on food, while Lord Grimond's column is the second best thing in the *Daily Telegraph*. Mr Joe Ashton has the common touch.

Fewer Conservatives can write. But Christopher Patten, Ian Gilmour and Philip Goodhart are worthy of a place in the Commons first eleven. Mr Eric Heffer used to have a weekly column in *The Times*. Any halfway articulate MP who can put pen to paper, can command the occasional column in the 'heavies', although the most profitable thing to do is to write for the populars, which now provide entertainment of a sort and not news of a kind; readership is high, and fees even higher. But invitations to perform are usually kept for national figures such as Dr David Owen or for Scots populists with a ready line in moral disapproval and a taste for solutions.

Conservatives should be wary of writing books. It is bad enough to be known to read them. But Mr Robert Rhodes James is perhaps our most distinguished historian, and Sir Ian Gilmour has no peer as a political scientist. Mr Jeffrey Archer is proof of the proposition that in each of us lurks one bad novel, but he, at least, had the courage of his convictions. Lord Bruce Gardyne was a well known scribbler until he accepted office at the hands of Mrs Thatcher, after which he slipped into obscurity, and published nothing, save for his private correspondence. He now worries about the state of the Nation on behalf of the commuters of Kent, Surrey and Sussex. I have written the above not to boast, but to show that in what passes for today's literary talent, we politicians can just about hold our own.

Of course, exposure carries with it the risk of indiscretion. In the autumn of 1983 I described Mrs Thatcher as 'the Great She Elephant' (in Swaziland it is a term of affection, even admiration) in the *Listener* piece about the Labour Party in conference in Harrogate which I have already quoted. This would have passed unnoticed, save for modish parsons married to Laura Ashley, had I not travelled north to appear on Tyne-Tees television. It is a mistake to appear late at night on a bad programme. Boredom can lead to carelessness. Miss Gillian Reynolds brought up the matter, and my acknowledgement of authorship (and, it is true, a little embellishment) was smartly sent off to the press by the only member of the company's staff paid to keep awake. Twenty-four hours later my compliment was all over the newspapers. It is curious how unpredictable the national press is. A remark or opinion which some might regard as merely pert, and others as outrageous, can either pass without notice, or, for no apparent reason, become the subject for leader comment. 'The Great She Elephant' was not meant to be a physical description — Mrs Thatcher is a handsome woman — but a dart fired in her direction. The Conservative Party *is* a tribe, and my description *is* precisely the same as the title bestowed upon an African equivalent of the Queen Mum: but I was also annoyed by two speeches the Prime Minister had made in Canada during which she had 'talked up' the Cold War in a way that could only help recruit new members for the Peace Movement. Thank God that since the autumn of '83 both President Reagan and the Prime Minister have changed their tune.

The pink slips with their promise of pounds sterling and the retainer paid by great national newspapers, have, I suppose, made some contribution towards the decline of the Chamber. Perhaps it is just time, but I do find that the 'great' Parliamentary occasions are rarely, if ever, that. Events which are talked up by the press and television are, more often than not, damp squibs, while the great speech seems, like Tasmanian tigers, to have almost completely disappeared. On his day, the best performer in the Commons is Michael

Foot, who usually speaks well, even when the circumstances have been, from his point of view, far from propitious. At his best, and when he can attack, he is superb, passionate yet coherent, witty and moving. And he speaks without notes. I think his speech winding up the No Confidence debate in May 1979 was the finest I have heard, a pleasure which makes up for much that has been turgid, some of which has been contributed by myself.

Television and radio, to say nothing of the contribution to the *Daily Telegraph* or to the *Guardian*'s 'Agenda' page, have conspired to take the older hands out of the Chamber, our places having been taken by the ranks of the newly-elected. And our contributions, with their emphasis upon brevity, have reinforced that tendency within the Chamber to inform rather than to enthuse. All too often the backbencher does not attempt to debate but clings to his text as if it were a life raft, unable or unwilling to plunge in. It is a strain to sit in the Chamber, with no certainty of being called upon to speak (unlike the Lords), from three thirty until say eight fifteen, listening to the contributions of your colleagues, helpless to prevent the theft of your better arguments, watching the number of MPs present dwindle to a half dozen seated on either side, when you are called. At a steady rate of ten to a dozen speeches a year, speeches which never exceed ten minutes and are often even shorter, I do not think I have ever spoken to a House which contained more than a hundred members. Fifteen to twenty would be the average figure. And the old courtesy of listening to the speech that follows yours is fast disappearing. The House is fairly interested in the two front bench speeches, assuming the debate to be one of importance. The front bench is then followed by two speeches from either side which are delivered by people of importance like Mr David Steel or Mr Francis Pym. After they have done, it is tea and buns, and the devil take the rest of us.

But if the backbenchers are bad enough, frontbenchers are worse. How often do they stand on one leg before the dispatch box, hunched over their text, which has been written for them by their private office, the burden of which they proceed to gabble, pausing only to scratch their private parts. I would rather have two teeth out than listen to some Ministers of the Crown.

A leader page article in the *Daily Telegraph* on a subject of current political importance is not only rewarding to write, it is read. A speech in *Hansard* is read by a handful only. An interjection at Question Time can gain the attention of the political scene writers, although it is not an hour for the sensitive, reminding me as it does of Percy Lubbock's dictum that civilisation, rather than being long established, has only just begun. Participation is the only way you can win a mention in the columns of the kind written so engagingly by Messrs Frank Johnson, Godfrey Barker, Michael White and James Naughtie, those gadflies who, striving desperately for effect, spend the hour between the end of an exquisite light lunch and a cup of china tea, pleasuring themselves in the Press Gallery. Question Time is often noisy, ridiculous and uninformative, and, in my view, should be avoided. To those delicate listeners who have expressed shock, even dismay, at what they hear of it on the radio, I can only murmur that they should have dropped in on the happy hour before we knew we were being broadcast. All this being said, the strain, the boredom, the disregard, I am sure that to make a great speech in the House of Commons, to be listened to by a rapidly filling and attentive House, to have been able to make them laugh and to have put your point across, and then to have received the genuine congratulation of friend and foe must be the most marvellous thing to have had happen. I would rather that than a hundred pieces in the press.

As for the Commons being televised, I am reluctantly in favour. There is a risk it might turn Dennis Skinner into the Nation's Sweetheart, but it is a risk I am willing to take. If the Commons is shown on the box, it will certainly encourage MPs to make more use of the Chamber, and by focusing attention upon it, strengthen its power vis à vis the Government, at the price, perhaps, of shocking the more sensitive viewer who mistakes the House of Commons for a Council of the Nation.

11   The Longest Hijack in the World

Looking back, the period from June 1970 to June 1979, when the Conservatives were returned after the twin defeats of 1974, was one of transition as the Conservative Party took on the colour of the woman who was elected its leader in the Peasants' Revolt of 1975. On my return in June 1970, after six years in the wilderness, I found the party somewhat changed: less patrician; the higher proportion of the ambitious middle class making competition for promotion more severe. On the Sunday before polling day, the *Sunday Express* tipped me for office, yet another example of the inability of that great paper to get things right. The three and a half years of the Heath Government was dominated by the campaign to win entry into Europe; the Prime Minister's mistiming of the February 1974 election date (for which he was obliged, quite properly, to take the blame, despite the urgings of the overwhelming majority of his backbenchers who saw a chance for electoral smash and grab), sealed his political fate. Defeat at a second election was inevitable. That being so it was only a matter of time before a challenge was mounted to Ted Heath's leadership. It came, and he lost, in the greater part due to the twin election defeats; in the smaller, to his failure to exercise the political arts. I will give one example, unimportant in itself, but one which must have been repeated many times.

At the end of October 1974, having survived, without difficulty, my third election in Aldershot, I joined Jim Prior, Tony Buck and David Walder for dinner in the House. Halfway through the beef, Ted Heath came into the dining room. He approached our table and spoke to Jim Prior, an old friend. The conversation was prolonged, but not by one word or gesture did he acknowledge Walder, Buck or myself, three 'moderate' MPs who had just returned from fighting an election under his banner. When he had gone Jim Prior, recognising Ted's failure to acknowledge us, said 'What can I do with him?' In the event Ted probably received three out of four votes, but he did not get mine; I voted for Margaret Thatcher on both ballots.

I did not do so out of pique. At least, I would like to think so. I offer the story of the dinner party conversation that did not take place only as an example. I wish I had voted for him; there is something rather splendid, in retrospect, about Heath's contempt for the political arts. If only, however, he had practised them.

The party did not vote for Margaret, they voted against Ted Heath. Had Willie Whitelaw challenged Heath on the first ballot, he would have won; so, too, would Edward du Cann. Heath's defeat was the result of a conspiracy launched by the officers and the executive of the 1922 Committee, who, for days after the two ballots, swaggered about the House like so many Portuguese army officers after the fall of Caetano. Regimes are rarely as robust as they seem. A combination of events, in particular the party's humiliation at the hands of Joe Gormley's miners, taken together with the umbrage of the large number of people, many but not all of whom were on the right of the party, whom Ted had offended, was more than enough to make his defeat inevitable. The only surprising thing was that he should have been replaced by Margaret Thatcher.

After the second ballot when she defeated Willie Whitelaw by 146 votes to 79 (Howe and Prior each got nineteen), the party met at the ballroom of the Europa Hotel to confirm her in office. The chair was taken by Quintin Hailsham, flanked by Reggie Maudling who was referred to by the chair as 'Reg', which took us somewhat by surprise. Hailsham and Maudling both said nice things about Ted (who had gone to Spain), but a letter from Heath was read out in which he hinted darkly at the difficulties facing country and party. Margaret's accession was then proposed by Hailsham, Whitelaw, and, finally, by two big-wigs from the National Union whom Hailsham almost forgot. Humphrey Atkins, the Chief Whip, was then despatched to bring the bride to the altar to tumultuous applause. It was all rather moving;

Geoffrey Howe told me that he had been near to tears. So began the longest political hijack in history.

Love her or loathe her, and few are dispassionate about her, there can be no doubt that she has been responsible for a sea change; her Premiership has been the most radical, and, in many respects, the most remarkable, since the end of the Second World War. She may even win a third general election running. She has had more than her share of luck (with enemies like Galtieri and Arthur Scargill, who needs friends?), but it would be churlish to make too much of that. She owes her success, and who can deny that she has come to dominate British politics, to the power of her will. And she has, in the meantime, locked up the Conservative Party, and thrown away the key.

What sort of woman is she? I cannot claim to know her. I can count the occasions on which we have exchanged words on the fingers of one hand. But I have sat neither at her feet nor on her head, although if I had to choose, I would prefer to do the latter. I find her stridency unattractive and her self-righteousness unappealing. She is a zealot whose fundamentalist beliefs were not, at the time of her election to the leadership of the party, as widely known as they are today. I voted for her at the time; a fact which some may find surprising, but then so did others, such as Norman St John Stevas on the second ballot, and Sir Peter Tapsell on both. But who can deny the extent of her success? She has, by exercising the politics of exclusion, rid herself of her enemies, at least in the Cabinet; she dominates the Commons Chamber and, despite a growing unrest among backbenchers, retains the support of the majority of her party. Mrs Thatcher is a woman of common views but uncommon abilities.

Mrs Thatcher is not so obvious at Westminster as the outsider might imagine. There is always the twice-weekly Prime Minister's questions for those who like that sort of thing, but for those who do not, the party leader is not much in evidence. One of the hazards, it is true, of life at Westminster is the Prime Ministerial convoy. The most self-effacing MP is in danger of being run down by it. He may gingerly emerge from his room only to be trampled under foot by a posse led by the determined figure of Mrs Thatcher who passes down the corridor in a cloud of powder blue. In step behind her are two apparatchiks, bearing files, and bringing up the rear, the tall figure of St Michael Allison, her PPS. Faced by this juggernaut, some fall to their knees, others take refuge within the nearest doorway. There is, too, as I have said, the possibility that she may join your table at lunch or dinner. If she does, take my tip and do not sign the bill, an act of convenience which incurs a minuscule financial penalty. Those who have been seen to sign have incurred the full force of her disapproval. That way lies national penury.

Many would forgive the Prime Minister had she a sense of humour, but she has none. A former Cabinet Minister, who has now gone on to his reward, was understood to have said, after a particularly disputatious cabinet meeting, 'What can you do with a woman to whom you cannot make love, and cannot make laugh?' There is an earnestness, a tendency to take herself too seriously which, when combined with a will of iron and the physical stamina of a long distance runner, makes her nearly impossible to 'manage'. Countless hours have been spent arguing her out of fixed, but untenable, positions.

Her sex has been of great advantage to her. The grander sort of Tory, faced with a tiresome woman, has long swopped her for another; but here it has been Mrs Thatcher who has been doing the swopping. Englishmen, and not only the traditional sort (many of whom only met their mothers for the first time when they came of age) have been placed at a disadvantage; and when 'the Lady', as she is often called, is not just difficult but convinced that hers is 'the way', that she, and her allies, are those to whom the truth has been revealed, then she becomes doubly formidable. Whatever the merits may be, she has had the better of the argument.

It is true that there are those within the Conservative Party who have never accepted her leadership. Given the fact that the party is a coalition of people in continual debate, she made do initially with a Cabinet that bore the stamp of her predecessor. But she soon made it clear that there were two categories of Tory: those who were 'one of us' (she is supposed to use the phrase 'not one of us' whenever Michael Heseltine is mentioned), and those who were, quite plainly, not. The fact that she has been able to exclude her 'enemies', or the bulk of them, is perfectly understandable;

123

she is, in fact engaged in a crusade of sorts, one that is not to everyone's taste. What is not so comprehensible is its wisdom. Those of us who have been cast into darkness were not impressed when, during her speech to the 1922 Committee at the end of 1984, she proclaimed, 'After all we are all Conservatives.' Some of us are clearly more Conservative than others.

Mrs Thatcher is a liberal, but not one of the Hampstead sort. She is the daughter of the redoubtable Alderman Roberts of Grantham who was a liberal of the nineteenth century kind, believing, as he did, in all the Victorian virtues, save for hypocrisy. But, whatever her views, she is not easy to find at Westminster. If you do not lunch or dine and escape the Prime Ministerial convoy, there are only the end of term meetings of the 1922 Committee, that Parliament of the Skimmed Milk, and the invitation to drinks or dinner at Downing Street. She has told us 'that my door is always open' but there is something faintly daunting about that invitation. I have attended meetings of the '22 which have been addressed by Harold Macmillan (like a University Historical Society), Sir Alec Douglas Home (like a meeting of the County Landowners' Association), Mr Edward Heath (like a City Dinner), and Mrs Thatcher (like Speech Day at a Girls' Public Day School Trust High School). I much preferred the first. Mrs Thatcher is addicted to the forefinger school of oratory, being inclined to hector. As for her parties, I cannot say as I have not been invited to any.

The Falklands War was the making of her. Before Galtieri chanced his arm, her standing in the public opinion polls was lower than that of any previous Prime Minister. 1981, with its running and very public Cabinet disputes over the course of her economic policy, was a bad year for her, and her position, which for a time looked shaky, was maintained in large part through the loyalty of Willie Whitelaw, the so called 'non-playing captain of the "wets" '. Victory changed it all.

When she spoke in the debate on the morning of Saturday April 3 1982, Mrs Thatcher made the worst speech of her career. The Falklands had been taken by force and she seemed shattered; and the lameness of her explanations was compounded by a silly attempt to blame the Labour Party

124

for what had happened. If anything, John Nott was worse. We listened to her in silence; she was in deep trouble, and the lobbies hummed with the prospect of her departure. But, by the end of June, everything had changed. Victory for British arms had changed her overnight from the party's biggest liability into its greatest asset. In the war against Argentina, Mrs Thatcher had found an event for which her talents were marvellously suited. She could externalise her enemies, and, by so doing, transform her standing.

As if by magic, her stridency, which had offended so many, was changed into resolution. Time may serve to change it back again. But victory confirmed in her supporters the image that they had held of her. The right of the party see her in almost Churchillian terms: vigorous, bent on reversing what they see as a continuing process of economic, social and political decline; a new broom to secure the counter-revolution. Her opponents in the Tory Party, on the other hand, shrink from her passion and mistrust her simplicity. They see her as a 'Lincolnshire edition of Reagan', a radical populist whose objectives fall way outside those held by the more traditional, moderate or paternalistic Tories who dislike her implacable zeal, a quality which remains profoundly untypical and antipathetic to mainstream Conservatism. The so called 'wets' (and the epithet is Mrs Thatcher's) have, despite the Falklands, regarded her principal contribution to be rhetoric and hold in distaste much of what she says, and, just as much, the tone of voice in which she says it.

But the 'wets' have been defeated. The extent of the defeat can be seen, at one level, in the remorseless rise in the unemployment figures; at another in the gilded list of names on the memorial to ex-Cabinet Ministers, a list which now includes: Lord Soames who was too grand; Mr Norman St John Stevas whose finely developed sense of ridicule was not to her taste ('the immaculate misconception'); Sir Ian Gilmour who had too many brains; Mr Mark Carlisle who did not punch his weight; and Lord Carrington whom she lost by accident but whose transfer to Brussels as Nato's Secretary General is proof of the proposition that an ill wind . . . The Cabinet of today contains only two known 'opponents': Mr Peter Walker who is licensed to dissent perhaps because he would be more formidable on the back than on the front bench, and Mr Michael Heseltine who tends not to be able to see a parapet without ducking below it.

Mrs Thatcher may well be difficult to deal with, but she also has some very considerable political strengths. As a populist, she feels intuitively that the British people are a good deal closer to a state of nature than many of us would readily admit. Her positions on law and order, capital punishment, permissiveness, denationalisation and the trade unions are the views of a great part of Britain. Her court admires her capacity to keep going into the small hours (a proclivity which may have saved her life at the Grand Hotel) with a singleness of purpose which can be alarming. She is inclined to strike attitudes, to shoot from the hip. Her admirers believe that she is the grit in the oyster; a necessary, if unwelcome challenge to the complacency which is the concomitant of power. She insists upon being taken at face value. As the leader of the party of the right, she has substituted populism for deference.

The Prime Minister has, in the past, been hostile towards Europe and has spoken as severely to foreigners as she has to her compatriots. She has been beastly to the Bank of England, has demanded that the BBC 'set its house in order' and still tends to believe the worst of civil servants in general and the Foreign and Commonwealth Office in particular. She cannot see an institution without hitting it with her handbag.

At times the despair of her colleagues, she has managed to retain the affection of the Conservative Party workers to an extent that Ted Heath could never manage. She has more support on the back benches, which is her natural constituency, than any other party leader I have known. She is free with honours, if somewhat generous to editors, and others, whom she considers friendly. She is not a good listener; she is kind, swift with the word that heals. But is it enough?

She does not cease to alarm me. Her attempt to tie the Conservative Party rigidly to the success of the free market, rather than being pragmatic and flexible, threatens to cut the party off from its past. Her thirst for conflict ('the enemies within') is socially divisive and politically unwise. The Tories are not the natural champions of the 'minimal state', and

126

fulsome support for a market economy has never been, until recently, a dominant feature of Conservative politics. Victory in the Falklands, which was the gift of our servicemen, served to restore national morale but its effect is rapidly wearing off. Mrs Thatcher has been, in party terms, a highly successful leader. But she has yet to become a national leader.

Since her second election victory, her touch has become even less predictable. There are calls for a return to Cabinet Government, although why anyone should wish to join a body which is summoned infrequently, is given a piece of the Prime Minister's mind when it does, and is then sent a bill for £23.50, as Mrs Thatcher does after the traditional

Cabinet eve-of-session dinner, is difficult to understand. The growth of ad-hoc Cabinet Committees, and, in particular, the enhanced position of her Cabinet Office, which is staffed largely with true believers, is serving to devalue the Cabinet itself. And, as is often the case with leaders in their second term, the intractability of problems at home serves to encourage the playing of a part on a wider stage. A passion for foreign affairs can develop, which, given President Reagan's amiable ignorance on many, if not most matters, makes him susceptible to the Prime Minister's ideas and the vigour with which they are expounded. Provided the objective remains to seek an honourable settlement with the East which will preserve both our security and our freedoms, few will complain.

I have watched Mrs Thatcher from afar for ten years. If she is vulnerable, it is to mockery. Her opponents make the mistake of taking her on, of trying to shout her down. My advice to Messrs Kinnock, Owen and Steel is to exchange the bludgeon for the rapier, to try ridicule. As for those of us within the Conservative Party with whom she does not see eye to eye, we must fight our corner with a view not to her conversion but to securing an eventual successor more to our taste. In the meantime, we should strive to soften some of the asperities.

12   A Word to the Wise

If we were to divide Conservative MPs into workers, peasants and intellectuals, I would fit uncomfortably into the third class. The workers have steadily replaced the peasants, as accountants wearing Conservative Club ties have been adopted in safe seats in place of the Knights of the Shires with their Trumper's haircuts and places in the country. The intellectuals have changed too; the sophists, economists and calculators, sailing under Freidmanite colours, having been wafted into places of power by the hot breath of the prevailing orthodoxy. Mrs Thatcher has personally ensured that the representatives of her sort of thinking command the senior posts in the party.

Mrs Thatcher has claimed frequently to be a 'conviction politician'. But what does it mean? It might mean that she holds strongly to carefully-thought-out views. What is more likely is that her heart controls her head. Throughout the years of her Premiership she has taken on board a fistful of simple beliefs, beliefs which stem either from her own Poujadist background (hence the oft repeated parallels between the family's housekeeping and that of the nation) or from her own experience of politics before 1975. For example, Britain needs the 'great' put back, inflation is too high, the trade unions are too powerful and the State too large.

And there are other convictions which have served to colour her party: that civil servants are idle, and that there are too many of them, some of whom hold unpalatable views, foreigners are unreliable and coloured foreigners are on the scrounge. Her intuitions, her 'convictions' have been buttressed by everything and everyone who is generally associated with what has come to be called 'Thatcherism' — monetarist doctrine, Professor Hayek, Milton Freidman,

Peter Bauer, and privatisation. All this has been built into a body of doctrine, complete with sacred flame.

The Conservative Party is still some way from being a cult in the Californian style. But we have been encouraged to believe that virtually everything that has been done by post war Conservative Governments was mistaken, and that it is only since 1975, the Peasants' Revolt, that the party has followed the path of true Conservatism. We are urged to follow our leader back into the nineteenth century in search of eternal truths.

This re-writing of recent history has had to be taken beyond the years of Ted Heath's Government in which Mrs Thatcher and Sir Keith Joseph served without demur, into a more general condemnation: to the true believer the post-war years have been ones of ever rising inflation and ever increasing deficits, the results of consensus Governments building on the 1944 political settlement. Neither proposition is demonstrably true; for much of the fifties and sixties inflation was negligible, and Governments ran a surplus every year from 1950 to 1974. Of such assertions myths are made; just as it has been the task of Saatchi and Saatchi to transmute Mrs Thatcher's dogmatism into resolution, a more marketable idea.

Mrs Thatcher owes much to Gordon Reece, a magician whose powers include, so it has been reported, the ability to make the Prime Minister laugh. He was responsible for persuading her to lower her voice by half an octave, and to adopt the throaty whisper which she assumes when asked a question about unemployment. His real skills, however, lie in his anticipation of what will be of interest to the popular press, and the good relations which he has so carefully cultivated with editors. Mrs Thatcher's populism carried the populars in both '79 and '83, but it now seems, if both the *Daily Mail* and *Express* are a guide, that the bottom end of Fleet Street will be harder to seduce in '87 or '88. Reece is an associate of Lord McAlpine, the party's Treasurer — the two are inseparable — whose technique is not always to the taste of the party's professionals. But they admire the length of his cigars and his passion for good champagne. Acute and personable though he is, I very much doubt if any other

Tory Prime Minister of recent years would have given him the time of day.

But what advice can I give to the younger Tory MP who wishes to rise within his party? In order to succeed in our party the backbencher must be as wise as a dove and as innocent as a serpent. He will, of course, have already recognised that what the party is presently suffering from is an addiction to an *idée en marche*, and he should promptly join the back of the column. Not to be a monetarist in today's party is to suffer from a severe handicap, it is the political equivalent of being young, black and unemployed. He should model himself either upon Mr John Stanley or Mr Nigel Lawson.

To those who cannot bring themselves to go quite as far, I shall offer some good advice. Harold Macmillan once said that there were only two rooms worth visiting, the Smoking Room and the Chamber. In the Smoking Room can be found comfort and camaraderie; in the Chamber a chance, at least, to make a mark. Politics is a performing art and it is important to speak well. Take lessons. Humming, Hawing and Hesitation are the three Graces of contemporary Parliamentary oratory. If you cannot be witty, then at least be brief. Do not neglect Prime Minister's Questions where a well timed soft ball is never unwelcome. Plunge in, and do not permit ignorance to inhibit your contribution.

Here I should strike a note of warning. Do not become a bore. There are some Members who make themselves foolish by making themselves available for comment on any subject whatsoever, the purveyors of the instant quote. It can truly be said of one or two of the better known Tory backbenchers that no cause was ever finally lost until X had made it his own.

How best to cope with Mrs Thatcher? She is reported to have once said that she takes ten seconds to make up her mind about a person, and 'rarely, if ever, do I change my mind'. If she has a weakness it is for shopkeepers, which probably accounts for the fact that she cannot pass a branch of Marks and Spencer's without inviting its manager to join her private office. Don a light brown, knee-length jacket into the breast pocket of which you have stuffed an assortment of

RT Hon
Nigel
Knowall M.P

OPINIONS
ON CURRENT
TOPICS

INSERT
2 X 50p
AND
LISTEN

pens and pencils and stand in the Lobby wringing your hands. This may lead to an order. It could also, given the uncharitable nature of the Palace of Westminster, get your name into the papers.

But something more may be called for. Keeping in mind that you have only ten seconds in which to make your mark, I suggest that the ambitious Member take advantage of her presence at lunch to join her at table. Sooner or later there will come a pause into which you should inject the following, delivered with resolution. 'Francis Pym, one of us, he isn't.' This message, capable as it is of many interpretations, will lead inevitably to an invitation to a wine and cheese given by the Conservative Philosophy Group, the home of the finest, if not the freest, spirits in our great party since the days of Balfour, where you will find yourself treading water in the company of Sir James Young, Lord Everett of Wembley and Sir Alfred Marks. If you are lucky you may even win the raffle.

The Conservative Philosophy Group is but one of several such unofficial bodies through membership of which your friends, and enemies, can get some idea of where you stand. Sir Patrick Wall recruits for those who would keep the party right wing: Sir William van Straubenzee does as much for the moderates. Nick's Diner is a club where the 'wets' meet to eat humble pie. At the time of the annual elections to the party's committees, two rival bands led by Mr George Gardiner and Colonel Mates organise support for right and left wing candidates respectively. Do not muddle up the Morrisons. Morrison *père* is now in the Lords as Margadale. In the sixties he was Chairman of the 1922 Committee, where he exercised the happy affectation of the very rich by driving a pre-war Morris Eight. As for the Morrison *fils,* Peter is of the right and Charlie very much of the left. But, on reflection, my advice to the ambitious is to avoid commitment; find the party's centre of gravity and sit on it.

But there are few short cuts. The road to the top of the Tory Party passes through the Whips' Office. Those who wish to gain life must first lose it. Make your number with the Chief, which can best be done by congratulating him on the quality of his speeches. Eschew flippancy, at all costs. For example, it just will not do to give, in answer to a question slyly posed by your Area Whip, 'Incidentally, who do you think is the greatest Prime Minister of the century?', the reply 'Victor Hugo, hélas.' It will not be understood, but it will not be appreciated either. You will be marked down as 'unsound'; and invited to join the Council of Europe.

Whatever the temptation, do not write for the newspapers, or appear on television, unless it is at the prompting of the Whips, for example in the comment spot after the seven o'clock news on Channel 4. Write only for the Eatanswill *Echo* or the *Conservative Newsletter,* published by Central Office. Do not let it be known that you keep a diary. Follow my advice and the ambitious MP will surely climb the ladder, rung by rung.

I confess that I am not perhaps the best person to offer advice on how to get on in the Tory Party. I, too, once wanted to become Parliamentary Secretary at the Department of Health and Social Security. But all I have received is a free transfer. I have, however, observed the Tory 'beast' at close quarters for a long time, and have affection for it. It includes some of the brightest and many of the best. It is also hugely entertaining, and, in its subtleties, more interesting perhaps than the other parties. My constituency chairman, Jack Bedser, an old friend who once worked for British Rail, and now labours in the National Trust's vineyard, once told me with reference to my *Observer* articles that he did not mind what I wrote, as long as I signed it. As for my life as a 'dissident' (the adjective is not mine) backbencher, I shall continue to order not from the set menu but from the à la carte. I would have liked office, but it has not come my way. At least some might still ask 'Why not?', which is greatly to be preferred to Tacitus's comment on the Emperor Galba, 'omnium consensu capax imperii nisi imperasset'.